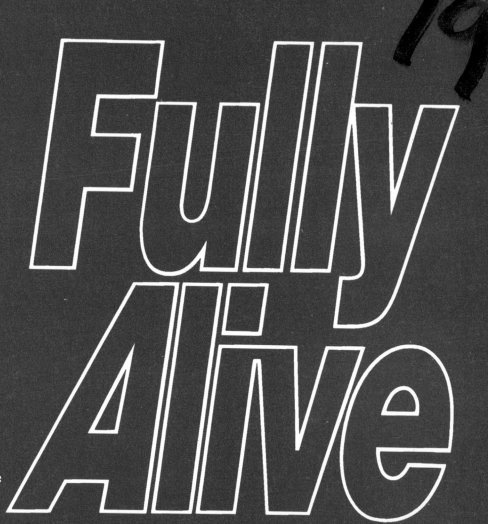

Fully Alive

A Family Life
Education program
sponsored by the
Ontario Conference of
Catholic Bishops

Maxwell Macmillan Canada

Maxwell Macmillan Canada, Inc.
1200 Eglinton Avenue East., Suite 200
Don Mills, Ontario M3C 3N1

IMPRIMATUR: John A. O'Mara, D.D.
President of the Ontario Conference
of Catholic Bishops
Bishop of Thunder Bay, Ontario

GENERAL EDITOR: Sylvia Santin
MANAGING EDITOR: Patrick Gallagher
DESIGN: Brant Cowie/ArtPlus Limited
ART DIRECTION: Lorraine Smith/ArtPlus Limited
PAGE MAKE UP: Valerie Phillips/ArtPlus Limited
PRODUCTION CO-ORDINATION: Gaynor Fitzpatrick

Canadian Cataloguing in Publication Data
Main entry under title:

Fully alive

For use in grade 7.
ISBN 0-02-953574-3

1. Family – Juvenile literature.   2. Sex
instruction for children – Religious aspects –
Catholic Church.   3. Catholic Church – Doctrines –
Juvenile literature.   I. Catholic Church.   Ontario
Conference of Catholic Bishops.

HQ10.F847 1991   306.85   C91-093388-X

Printed in Canada

 2 3 4 5   95 94 93 92

Table of Contents

Created and Loved by God

Then God said, "Let us make human beings in our image, after our likeness. . ."
CF. GENESIS 1:26

Who are you? What does it mean to be a person? These are the kinds of questions that are examined in Theme 1. First impressions, self-concept, personality, heredity, environment, and the limitations and choices that are part of each person's life are some of the topics you will explore. As you discuss the ideas in this theme, and learn more about yourself and others, you will also discover that you have been exploring a wonderful mystery—the mystery of the human person created in the image and likeness of God.

To Be A Person

Imagine that you have just walked into this classroom on a dull morning in November. Mr. Dryden's class of Grade 7 and 8 students are working on math problems. What are your first impressions of Bill, Mark, Tracey, Tina, Mai, Tom, and Angie?

As you know, first impressions can be very misleading. In order to know what kind of people Bill, Mark, Tracey, Tina, Mai, Tom, and Angie really are, you would have to spend a lot of time with them. You might also find it helpful to talk to other people who know them well.

Let's take a closer look at one of these students. Who is Tracey? What kind of a person is she?

A Portrait of Tracey

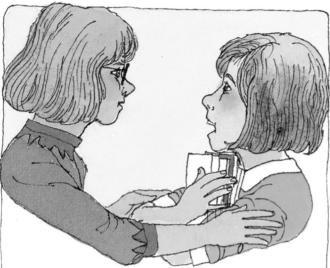

"I've known Tracey since third grade, and she's a really good friend. Sometimes we have long talks. Things aren't so good at home for me right now and Tracey's someone I can confide in."

"Tracey's an interesting person. I taught her last year so I think I know her quite well. She's an average student and would be much better if she put out more effort. Most of the time I feel that her heart isn't really in her work, except when it comes to writing. She has a wonderful talent that I would like to see her develop. Tracey is popular with the other students and I would describe her as a natural leader. If someone in the class has been treated unfairly, Tracey's the first one to mention it. I enjoy her as a student, and I know she cares about my opinion, but not enough to work harder. She has to find a reason inside herself."

"What's Tracey like? Well, she's very good at sports and everybody likes her. It's great when it's just Tracey and me, but when Angie's around, the three of us don't get along so well. Angie never wants to do anything I want to do and then Tracey gets in a bad mood."

You have seen Tracey through the eyes of her friends and her teacher. But what does Tracey have to say about herself?

"Who am I? I never used to think about it much, but that's changing. I also worry more, like what if there was a war, or about silly things, like what if I go to school and none of my friends will talk to me! Sometimes I talk to my mom about how I'm feeling, or sometimes I lie in bed and talk to God. There are a lot of things I don't understand, like why are there always wars and people fighting with each other.

"I hate the way I look. I feel like a giant. Except for Bill, I'm the tallest person in my class. My hair's dirty blonde and I wear glasses.

"School is all right. I know everyone wishes I'd work harder. I suppose I could do better but I'm not a brain like Angie, and besides, maybe I'm not as smart as Mr. Dryden thinks.

"I've always been good at sports, but I get really scared before a tryout. I don't want anyone to know I'm nervous, so I act like everything's all right.

"Things I like: writing poetry, sports, horses, reading a good book, my little sister, babysitting, summer.

"Things I DO NOT like: editing my writing, my older brother, being called stubborn, wearing glasses, being treated like a baby.

"It's not completely true that I don't like my brother, Chris. Sometimes we have a lot of fun together, but right now, he's in trouble with my parents all the time. He never comes in when he's supposed to, he skips school, and he's causing a lot of fights with Mom and Dad. When I tried to talk to him about it, he told me to butt out and mind my own business.

"I don't have big fights with my parents, just arguments about my messy room or sometimes my marks. Mostly we get along pretty well. Everyone says that I'm just like my father — big and stubborn. I'd rather look like my little sister, Sara, who looks just like my mother.

"I think I'd like to be a writer when I grow up. The only people who know that I want to be a writer are Mr. Dryden, my mom, and Angie. I can tell Angie things that I can't tell anyone else.

"My other best friend is Tina, but she's really different from Angie. They don't get along very well and I never know what to do. It's like I'm in the middle.

"I babysit almost every week-end and I'm saving my money for horse-back riding. I went to a riding program for one week last summer, and it was great. When I'm in high school I'd like to work at a riding camp. High school — I wonder what it will be like."

There are still some other people who can add to the portrait of Tracey.

"Tracey's changed a lot in the last year. She's more serious and she keeps more to herself. It may sound silly, but I miss the little girl who used to tell me everything. But sometimes we have wonderful talks — about the future, about the way I felt at her age, or about issues in the news.

"I know she's feeling awkward because she's grown so quickly. I keep telling her that in a few years she'll be more comfortable with her body, but I'm not sure she believes me.

"Ever since Tracey learned to talk, she's always been blunt. She says what she thinks. I admire that quality in her, but she needs to learn to be more tactful."

"Tracey and I are a lot alike, so it's easy for me to see her faults because they're mine too. She's independent and stubborn and when she suspects that you want her to do something, she's likely to want to do the opposite. But she stands up for her beliefs, and that's a fine quality. She's not easily led and has a lot of common sense.

"I'm proud of her accomplishments. She's a good athlete, and she won her school's public speaking contest for her grade. She worked hard on her speech and it showed. I wish she would put that much effort into all her work."

"Tracey's my big sister and I think she's a very good big sister. She hardly ever bosses me around. One time when she was in trouble because her room was messy, I cleaned it all up for her, and the next day she took me to a movie."

"Tracey's not speaking to me right now because I told her to mind her own business. When she gets mad, she stays mad. I tried to be nice to her yesterday, but she just ignored me."

You now have much more than a first impression of Tracey. If someone asked you, "Who is this person named Tracey?" you could answer. Or could you?

The Mystery of People

Did you notice the title of the section on page 2? What does it mean *to be a person*? In some ways, it might seem like a rather easy question to answer.

PERSON: A MEMBER OF THE SPECIES *HOMO SAPIENS*, THE MOST DEVELOPED OF ALL LIVING CREATURES; MEMBERS OF THIS SPECIES HAVE LARGE AND COMPLEX BRAINS, AND ARE CAPABLE OF RATIONAL THOUGHT AND SPEECH.

Another way to understand what it means to be a person is to listen to what people tell us about themselves. What people think and feel about themselves is called their *self-concept*.

Tracey's self-concept has been deeply influenced by what she believes other people think of her. People's opinions about us have a strong effect on the way we see ourselves.

But there is more to being a person than self-concept. No matter what your appearance, achievements, or talents, or the opinions of other people, you are, above all, a physical-spiritual creature who is loved by God. That will never change even though aspects of your life will change. Your spirit, or soul, gives life to your body and together with your body is you — a human person.

To be a person is to be a physical-spiritual creature made in the image of God. Our ability to know and to love, our concern for good and evil, and our freedom are human capacities that are Godlike. We can learn, ask questions, explore, and try to understand other people and the world we live in. We are free to make choices and decisions; we are free to act and we are responsible for our actions. Within us we have a sense of what is right and what is wrong, which is called conscience.

To be a person is to live in relationship with other people. God did not create us to be alone. It is an essential part of our human nature to live in community with others. The family is the first community where we learn about relationships, love, friendship, and cooperation.

To be a person is to experience limitations and failures as part of our lives. Our ability to know and to act freely, wonderful as it is, is limited. Although we are meant for friendship with God and each other, at times we ignore conscience and turn away from others and disobey God's laws. Sin affects all human communities from the smallest to the largest.

But to be a person is also to be so loved that God became one of us. Jesus Christ is our model for what it means to be a person. In Jesus Christ we find the way back to friendship with God and with others.

Above all, to be a person is to be a mystery. We can never know everything there is to know about anyone, including ourselves. The more we come to know someone, the more we sense something deep and wonderful — something beyond our ability to understand. We have come face to face with a mystery, the mystery of the human person, made in God's image. We are in the presence of the spirit of our Creator.

Different People, Different Styles

"He has no personality." "She has a great personality." "He has lots of personality." What *is* personality? Is it something that certain people have a lot of, and others, not very much? People often talk about personality as if it was something that we *have*, but personality is really something that we *are*.

Each one of us has a unique style of being a person. When we talk about personality we are really talking about this style — the physical, intellectual, social, emotional, and spiritual characteristics that distinguish each of us from all others. Personality has a strong influence on our relationships with other people, on the way we interpret our experience, and at times even on the way we think.

Serious, shy, outgoing, lively, reliable, calm, anxious, reserved, impulsive, quiet, pessimistic, independent — these are only some of the many personality characteristics or traits that people demonstrate.

Personality is not the same thing as mood. Mood refers to the way a person feels at a particular time. Someone who is in a bad mood is feeling unhappy or angry at that time. This doesn't mean that the person has an unhappy or angry personality. In fact, it could be that he or she is rarely in a bad mood, but something sad or unfair has recently happened.

Sometimes we use the word *moody* to describe someone who is frequently sad, upset, or angry. In this case, moodiness is one of the person's personality traits. People whose moods change rapidly — one minute they're up, the next minute they're down — are often described as changeable or unpredictable.

Exploring Your Personality

Thousands of years ago the Greeks developed a theory of personality. They thought there were four basic temperaments or personality types, which were determined by the relative proportion of four body fluids — blood, phlegm, black bile, and yellow bile.

Over the years, there have been many theories about personality. Some researchers have tried to develop accurate ways to describe and measure personality traits. Others have examined the influences of environment and genetic inheritance on behaviour. Thousands of books have been written about personality since the days of the ancient Greeks, but there is still much that we do not know. The unique style of each individual is difficult to describe, and more difficult to explain. Theories about personality contribute to our understanding of ourselves and others, but they can never fully explain the mystery of the human person.

One aspect of personality that has interested researchers is the direction of an individual's energies and interests. Some people seem to be directed outward toward activities and relationships, while others are directed inward toward ideas and their own thoughts and feelings. This aspect of personality is often referred to as *extraversion* (directed outward) and *intraversion* (directed inward). Extraversion/intraversion is something like a "supertrait" since other

- melancholic (black bile): tends to see the dark side of any situation

- choleric (yellow bile): is excitable and gets angry very easily

- sanguine (blood): tends to see the bright side of any situation

- phlegmatic (phlegm): remains calm in most situations

personality characteristics are often associated with it. Descriptions of extraverts often include these words: *active, outgoing, talkative, easygoing,* and *sociable.* People who are intraverts are usually described as *calm, even-tempered, reliable, thoughtful,* and *controlled.*

Very few people are complete extraverts or complete intraverts. The most accurate way to think of this aspect of personality is as a tendency. Most people are inclined to be either somewhat extraverted or somewhat intraverted.

You might be wondering whether this aspect of personality will change as you go through adolescence. To some extent, this will depend on you. The better you understand and accept yourself, the more realistic you can be about your strengths and weaknesses. If, for example, you have always been a quiet intravert, you may decide that you would like to be a little more active and outgoing. On the other hand, if you have always been a talkative extravert, you may want to learn to be a better listener or to spend a little more time alone, getting to know yourself. Whether you will be successful depends on several factors: Are your goals realistic? Are you willing to make a conscious effort? Do you have a plan of action?

Now that you know a little bit more about personality, look back to the opening paragraph of page 9. Why are some people described as having a "lot" of personality and others, "no" personality?

Everyone has a personality. That's part of being human. Some people's traits, however, are more obvious than others. Strong extraverts, for example, are easily noticed. They bounce around, are involved in many activities, share their thoughts and feelings easily, and always seem to be talking and laughing. Strong intraverts have just as much personality, but their characteristics are not as obvious. It takes longer to get to know someone who doesn't socialize a lot, smiles quietly instead of laughing out loud, and shares thoughts and feelings with only a few people.

Sometimes a particular personality type is highly valued by a certain group of people. For example, many North American teenagers admire people who are lively and sociable. But the qualities of thoughtfulness and peacefulness are equally important and valuable, even though they do not always get the recognition they deserve.

Life would be very dull without the wonderful mixture of traits that each person has. It is part of God's marvelous design that the world is filled with unique individuals, each with the potential to have a "great" personality.

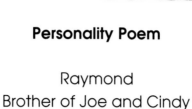

Personality Poem

Raymond
Brother of Joe and Cindy
Son of Jean and Al
Moody, unpredictable, loyal, complicated
Who loves — daydreaming, books, music
Who feels — confused, happy, sad
Who needs — friends, a place to be alone, books to read
Who looks forward to — being grown up, driving a car, being in high school
Who prays for — my family, my friends, peace.

How Did You Get to Be You?

If you think back to when you were in grade one, you will realize how much you have changed. You are still the same person, but your appearance is quite different, your personality traits are more distinct, and you have had a lot more experience at being the person you are. Your appearance will continue to change (especially in the next few years), your personality will develop, and as each day goes by you will learn more about yourself and others. You have come a long way, and you have a long way to go. It's a good idea to stop for a minute to think about how you got to be the person you are.

Your Heredity

In every cell of the human body, except for mature reproductive cells (ova or sperm cells), there are 46 chromosomes, arranged in 23 pairs. Along each tiny, thread-like chromosome lie thousands of even tinier genes. Genes are chemical structures, and each one contains a specific piece of genetic information that was inherited at the time of conception. It is estimated that there are over one million genes in each cell of the body. Among the physical characteristics that are determined by genes are hair, skin, and eye colour, body build, facial features, height, and blood type.

Everyone has at least two genes for each characteristic, one inherited from the mother, one from the father. But because the sperm and ovum each have only 23 chromosomes (one from each of the 23 pairs), the mother and father can pass on only the genetic information that happens to be on those 23 chromosomes. This is why children from the same family have a different genetic make-up, even though they share the same parents. Each mature ovum and sperm cell is unique in the genetic information it carries.

At the time of conception, the 23 chromosomes from the ovum and the 23 chromosomes from the sperm come together and arrange themselves in pairs. In this way the new human life begins as a single cell with 46 chromosomes, half from the mother and half from the father. All of the genetic information contained in the ovum and sperm is passed on, but in some cases not all of it will be apparent in the child.

For example, people look at Angie and Mark and see that they both have brown eyes. But if they could look inside the cells of Angie's body, they would see that she also carries genetic information for blue eyes. Mark's cells, however, have genetic information for brown eyes only. How did this happen?

The gene that determines brown eyes is called a *dominant* gene and is 'stronger' than the gene for blue eyes, which is called a *recessive* gene. Angie inherited a dominant gene for brown eyes from her father, and a recessive gene for blue eyes from her mother. Whenever there is a pair of genes, one dominant and one recessive, the dominant gene will be expressed. So Angie has brown eyes, but she carries in her cells the genetic information for blue eyes. If she has children, she could pass her recessive gene for blue eyes to them. If her husband also passes on a gene for blue eyes, then their child will be blue-eyed. Mark, however, can only pass on a gene for brown eyes, since he received genes for brown eyes from both his mother and his father.

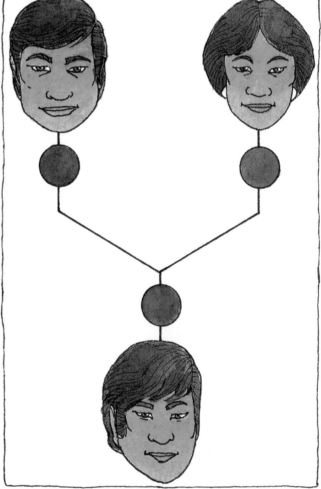

Have you ever noticed that some people have distinct ear lobes (detached) and others seem to have almost no ear lobes at all (attached)? The gene for detached ear lobes is dominant, and the gene for attached ear lobes is recessive. If you have attached ear lobes, you inherited a recessive gene for this trait from both of your parents.

Can you roll your tongue? The gene for tongue rolling is usually dominant so if you can't do it, you probably inherited a recessive gene from both of your parents.

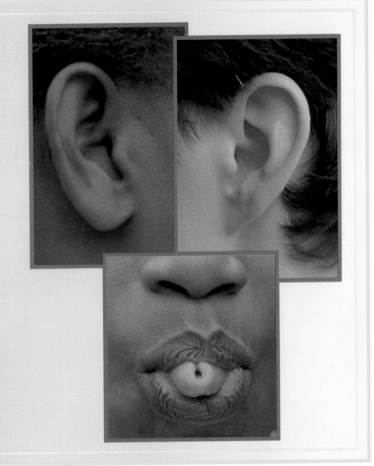

As well as inheriting physical characteristics from our parents, we also inherit talents and personality traits. But inheriting a talent or personality trait is not like inheriting blue eyes or type O blood. Eye colour and blood type are fixed characteristics; they do not change. If you are a blue-eyed person, you will always be a blue-eyed person.

An inherited talent for music, art, or mathematics is not a fixed characteristic. Tom inherited a talent for music; he has the *potential* to be a good musician. Whether or not he becomes a good musician depends on many things. His inherited talent for music is a "maybe," a future possibility. In the same way, an inherited personality trait such as shyness is not a fixed chararacteristic. What is inherited is a *tendency* to be shy.

An important part of the story of how you got to be you is found in the genes that you inherited from your parents, grandparents, and great-grandparents. But important as this inheritance is, it is only part of the story.

Your Environment

From the moment you were conceived, you have lived in an *environment*. Anything that is outside of you and has an effect on you and your development is part of your environment. Since environment includes so many conditions, it is useful to divide it into two categories: physical environment and social environment.

Physical Environment

The first physical environment for each person is the uterus. From the time of conception, outside influences begin to play a part in our lives. This is why it is especially important for pregnant women to get adequate rest, eat nourishing foods, and avoid alcohol, cigarettes, and unnecessary drugs.

The weather, the food you eat, the music you listen to, and even the colour of paint on the walls of a room are all part of your physical environment. Long rainy periods without sunshine make many people feel depressed and tired. Not eating regularly or eating too much junk food is hard on a person's body. If you spend a lot of time in an environment that is extremely hot, cold, noisy, crowded or dirty, it can have an impact on your emotional and physical health.

Heredity and environment come together in one unique person and *interact* with each other. *Interact* means that heredity and environment have an effect on each other. Hay fever is a good example of this interaction. If you have hay fever, it means you inherited a tendency to allergies and have developed a sensitivity to a tiny part of the physical environment called pollen. Pollen makes you sneeze, gives you red eyes and a runny nose, and makes you feel awful. Your environment is interacting with your heredity and influencing you in a very unpleasant way.

In order to relieve your stuffy head, you may have to make some changes in your environment. Perhaps you will avoid going outside except when necessary. You may decide to take allergy pills or shots. Your inherited tendency to allergies is now having an influence on your environment.

The First Environment

In his book, *The Secret Life of the Unborn Child,* Dr. Thomas Verny tells a story about a man who could never understand why the cello line from certain pieces of music, which he had never seen before, seemed so familiar to him. When he mentioned this experience to his mother, she was able to explain it. His mother was a cellist, and the musical scores that were so familiar to him were those that she had practised while she was pregnant with him.

As we learn more about the development and abilities of the unborn child, we also discover new facts about the uterus as an environment. It is not quiet, but is filled with the noise of the mother's digestion, her heartbeat, her voice, other voices from people nearby, and sounds — like music. The baby hears clearly from the sixth month of development, and is disturbed by sudden loud noises, which he or she reacts to by kicking furiously. Emotions from the mother such as strong anger or fear also prompt the kicking reaction. Because babies are so sensitive to their environment, some researchers are convinced that it is important for mothers to care for themselves, not just physically, but emotionally as well. A happy and relaxed mother, who has the support of a considerate husband, helps to create a peaceful and comfortable environment for her unborn child.

Adoption, Heredity, and Environment

Which is the most important influence on people — their heredity or their environment? This question has fascinated people for years. In recent years, most of the psychologists and medical researchers who study this issue like to point out that heredity and environment begin to interact from the moment we are born. Because of this interaction, it is almost impossible to separate these two influences.

Because they have not been raised by their birth parents, people who are adopted often wonder about their heredity. They may want to know about the medical background, appearance, interests, and talents of their birth parents. Nowadays, adoptive parents are much better informed than they were in the past about the birth parents, and can share this information with their adopted children. But there will still be some questions that remain unanswered. This is a serious concern for many adopted people.

But it is important for all of us to remember the immense contribution that environment makes to our identity — who we are now, and how we will develop in the future. Heredity is part of the picture, but it is environment that brings our genetic potential to life. Without nourishing food, shelter, warm clothes to wear, a loving family, friends to confide in, and the opportunity to learn, it would be very difficult for us to grow and develop and become the people God intended us to be.

Social Environment

In addition to the physical environment, you also live in a social environment, which is created by people. Each person who is part of your life, and especially those to whom you are close, contributes to your social environment. We know that social environments have a strong influence on each person, but this influence is much more complex and difficult to understand than the effects of the physical environment.

• Family

The first and most important social environment is the family. Our families influence our total development as people. This includes personality, achievements, beliefs, values, attitudes, and behaviour. Let's look at just one example of this powerful influence.

Earlier we talked about inherited tendencies and potential. Some people are born with the potential to be excellent athletes. At a very early age they show good coordination, balance, flexibility, strength, and endurance. But can we predict which, if any, of these athletically talented people will fulfill their potential and become an award-winning gymnast, a star football player, or a famous long-distance runner?

Family and friends are important examples of our social environment.

The family plays an important role in determining the answer to this question. For example, families might:

• frequently attend athletic events
• have no interest in sports
• be unable to afford sports equipment
• participate in a variety of sports activities
• encourage all family members to try their hardest at everything they do
• value doing well in school much more than athletic achievement.

The family, however, won't be the only influence on an athletic career. A person might get a lot of support and encouragement from the family, but discover that he or she doesn't like competition, or has too many other interests to spend the necessary time on training. Or it could happen that the family environment provides very little support for an individual, and yet that person still manages to become an outstanding athlete.

• Friends

Friends are also an important part of our social environment. The influence of friends is not as strong as that of family, but it becomes more powerful as we grow up. Friends introduce us to new interests, influence our attitude toward achievement, and have an effect on our values and behaviour.

Tracey behaves quite differently with her two best friends. With Angie, she tends to be more serious and enjoys talking about poetry and plans for the future. When she is with Tina, Tracey laughs a lot and talks about people in their class. You have probably had similar experiences. Different friends brings out different aspects of our personalities. In some cases, we behave better with some people, and worse with others.

As well as your family members and friends, there are various groups to which you belong — your classroom, school, parish community, the teams and clubs in which you are active, and the neighborhood community in which you live. Together, the people who belong to these groups create a social environment that has an influence on each of them.

For example, think about your classroom environment. Is the general atmosphere warm or cool? Is discipline a problem, or are most of the students well behaved? Do most students come from similar backgrounds and have similar experiences or is there a great variety of backgrounds and experiences? Each of these characteristics is an aspect of your classroom's social environment and has an influence on you and on every other student.

There is another important contributor to the social environment that people often talk about, and in some cases, worry about. The media — television, movies, videos, newspapers, magazines, radio — are created to inform and entertain us, but they also influence our opinions, attitudes, and values. Do you think these people have been influenced by the media? In what way?

"When I grow up I'm going to have a large house, a swimming pool, and at least three cars."

"The way to be popular is to drink and party."

"People have to get more serious about protecting the physical environment."

Your Experience in Your Environment

Did you know that at this point in your life you have been alive for over 100 000 hours? That's a lot of living. During these hours you have had thousands of experiences. Eating, sleeping, loving, learning, achieving, failing, celebrating, praying, working, being friends, belonging to a group, being left out, making plans, looking forward to something, being disappointed, being surprised — these are just a few of your life experiences. At various times you have felt happy, sad, lonely, excited, angry, frustrated, jealous, worried, guilty, bored, interested, hopeful, curious, and fearful. You have been very busy becoming the person you are.

All of these experiences are part of you. Among them, however, there are probably some that stand out in your mind because they were either very good or very difficult. A particularly wonderful birthday, an unhappy event in your family, a high mark on a school project, being blamed for something that you didn't do — these are the kinds of experiences that people remember.

We can deny our feelings.

When you have had a lot of fun, or worked hard and achieved a goal, you feel wonderful. Good experiences help people believe in themselves and look forward to the future.

Difficult or sad experiences can have the opposite effect. You fail an important test; you feel disappointed and upset, and wonder if you're stupid. Someone you care about very much is no longer part of your life. You feel sad and angry, and deep inside, you wonder if you are to blame. If you were a better person, would it have happened?

We all have times when it is hard to believe in ourselves. This experience is part of being human, and we have to find ways to cope with disappointments and failures, both small and large.

When we are very upset, hurt, and disappointed, it is often hard to believe that we will ever feel happy again. These are the times when we have to be honest about the way we feel, and talk to someone we trust. We need to share our experiences, and not just the good ones, with others. And above all, through good times and bad times, we need a strong relationship with God, who always believes in us.

We can blame others for the way we feel.

We can confide in people we trust.

We can turn our attention to other aspects of our lives.

Where Do You Go From Here?

As you think about your heredity and environment, you will discover that there are some aspects of your life over which you have no control. You did not choose your genes or your family. You may wish that you were taller, stronger, or smarter, that your parents were less strict, or that you had different brothers and sisters. Maybe you have hopes of being a famous singer even though you have no ear for music. Everyone daydreams once in a while about being a different person. But spending a lot of time wishing you were someone else doesn't get you very far.

You are meant to be the person that you are, with all your strengths, weaknesses, potential, and limitations. To accept yourself doesn't mean that you are unaware of your faults or spend all your time thinking about yourself. Self-acceptance means saying "yes" to the gift of being yourself, of being this unique person. This is what we mean when we say that God loves each of us. God says "yes" to us in this way.

Many people have contributed to your development as a person. By loving you, being honest with you, guiding you, and supporting you, they have made it possible for you to believe in yourself. There have also been times when people have disappointed you, failed you, and hurt you. They have made it difficult for you to believe in yourself. But important as other people are in your life, you are ultimately responsible for yourself and your growth. It is not a responsibility that you can give to someone else.

When you were a baby, you had little control over your life. With each passing year, you have played a larger and larger role in deciding what kind of person you want to be. The choices you make as you continue to develop will have an impact, not only on your own life, but on the lives of others. For you are part of the physical and social environment. You share the earth with others. You are a family member, a friend, a student in a classroom, and a resident in a neighbourhood. Above all, you are a member of the body of Christ, and are called to be a sign of God's love.

Along with every other person in the world, you have been given the capacity to know, to love, to choose, to act, and to seek what is good. You are also unique. Your personality, your experiences, and your potential are not exactly like anyone else's. There are limitations in your life just as there are in every life. You are not free to be anything you want. But you are free to make wise choices and decisions. You are free to develop the habits of self-honesty and self-discipline that will allow you to fulfill your potential. With God's help you are free to be you.

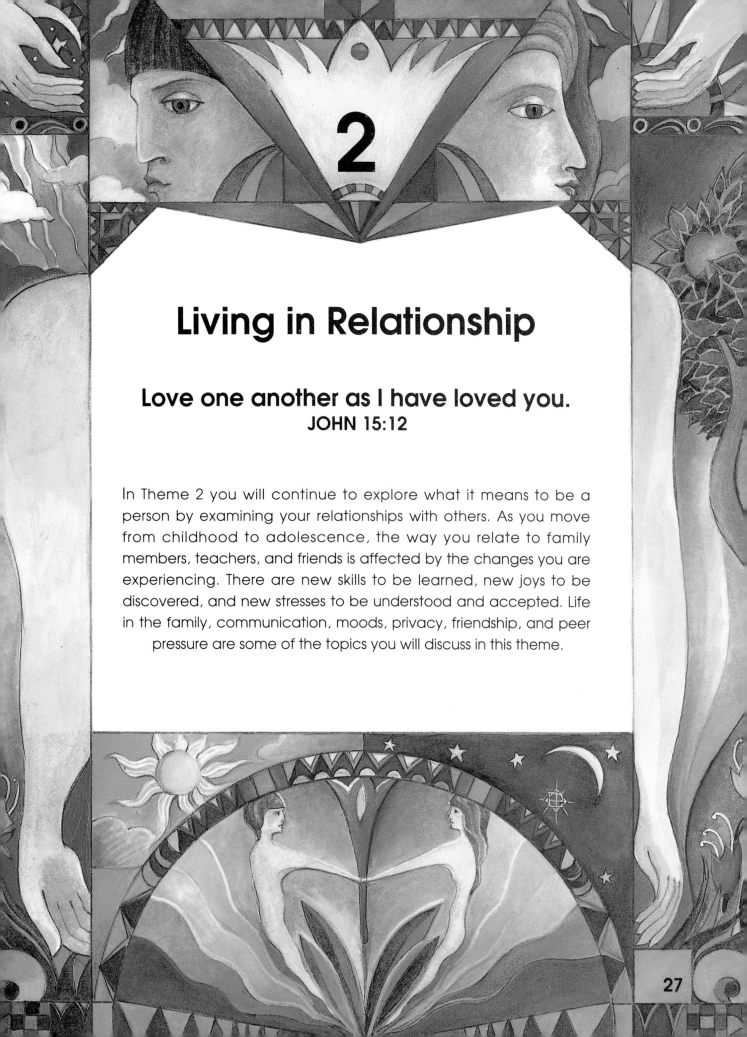

Living in Relationship

Love one another as I have loved you.
JOHN 15:12

In Theme 2 you will continue to explore what it means to be a person by examining your relationships with others. As you move from childhood to adolescence, the way you relate to family members, teachers, and friends is affected by the changes you are experiencing. There are new skills to be learned, new joys to be discovered, and new stresses to be understood and accepted. Life in the family, communication, moods, privacy, friendship, and peer pressure are some of the topics you will discuss in this theme.

All Kinds of Relationships

These scenes don't give you a lot of information about Tom, but they do provide a glimpse of a very important aspect of his life. Tom, like every other person, lives his life in relationship with other people. It is part of his human nature to be social, to seek contact with others, to be influenced by his relationships, and to have an influence on the people with whom he relates.

Describing Relationships

Relationships can be explored from many points of view, but there are three aspects that are particularly important to think about: intimacy, choice, and quality.

Intimacy: From Surface to Depth

• When Tom was in the market picking up groceries for his mother, he spoke briefly with the owner. He has pleasant memories of her, because when he was a little boy she used to give him candy or fruit when he came to the market with his mom or dad. Nowadays, he rarely sees her.

• Imagine that you run into someone who used to be in your class. This person's family moved several years ago, and even though you were fairly good friends, you haven't met since then. After chatting for a while, you exchange telephone numbers and make plans to get together.

• Bill and his father had a big argument before he left for school. It bothered Bill all day. He felt his dad was unfair, but he also knew that he said things that were hurtful. When Bill arrived home, he was relieved and disappointed that his dad wasn't home yet. He turned on the television, but the program didn't hold his interest. There was homework to be done, but he couldn't concentrate. Finally he decided to walk to the store. Maybe when he got back his dad would be home.

Three very different relationships — the first superficial, the last very deep, and the second somewhere in between. *Superficial* means "on the surface." Superficial relationships have very little effect on who we are as persons. They stay on the surface of our lives and do not touch us deeply. Sometimes a superficial relationship develops into a closer one. You meet someone, and you want to get to know that person better. You spend time together talking and sharing experiences. You learn more about each other, and the relationship grows. You develop loyalty and trust toward each other.

Our relationships with family members and close friends touch us deeply. They involve our feelings, thoughts, attitudes, and self-concept. These relationships are deeply personal because they have an effect on who we are as persons. That is why arguments with people we care about are so upsetting. The word *intimate* is another way of describing very close relationships. When you are intimate with another, you freely share yourself with that person. You are not afraid to talk about things that worry you or make you sad, or about how dissatisfied you are with yourself at times. You want to be understood, and to understand the other person.

Choice: Learning to Relate

People have many relationships they did not choose, including some of their most important ones. Tom, like you, was born into a family. He did not choose his parents, his sister or his brother. He did not choose Mr. Dryden as his teacher, or his next door neighbours. Yet in learning to relate to all of these people, and especially to his family members, Tom has been learning how to be a person. These relationships have taught him how to reach out, connect with other people, and make new friends.

Friendship is a relationship that we choose for ourselves. It is usually when people are about eleven or twelve years old that they first realize that being friends can involve more than playing together, sharing an interest, or belonging to the same team. They begin to look for friendships that are based on trust, acceptance, and appreciation. This kind of friendship is a choice, and requires effort and brings responsibilities.

Quality: Supportive relationships

If each person in the world was perfect, then our relationships would also be perfect. But we know that this is not the way things are. Tom, for example, has days when his relationship with his older sister is far from perfect. He hates being teased by her, and he knows that it drives her crazy if he hangs around when her friends are over.

We are all inclined to be selfish. When you were very young and someone called you selfish, it was probably because you wouldn't share your toys. A more adult way of understanding selfishness is that it is a refusal to give yourself to other people. Sometimes we are afraid to let people know who we are, and so we hesitate to share our thoughts and feelings. Or we forget that other people have feelings and we put someone down in order to put ourselves up. We are also inclined to worry about ourselves: Will I be left out? Do I belong? Do other people like me?

Part of the answer to these difficulties lies in learning to understand and accept ourselves, and we cannot do that alone. We need a relationship with God and with others to overcome our selfishness. It is through prayer, and through the acceptance, trust, forgiveness, and support we receive from our family members and friends that we become more loving people. We are still left with our faults, our fears, and our worries, but they no longer overwhelm us. Supportive relationships free us from our concerns about ourselves so that we can be more generous with others. Supportive relationships give us the confidence to offer other people acceptance, trust, forgiveness, and support.

A New Look At Relationships

It is natural that relationships change over time. This is especially true during the life stage of adolescence. Tom and his sister, for example, were very close when they were small children. Yet, for the past year, they have had difficulty finding a new way to be friends now that they are older. In a few years this problem may resolve itself, and they will again be able to enjoy each other's company.

If you can remember what you were like when you were only two or three years old, you will realize how much your family relationships have changed. At that age children depend on their parents for everything — a snack when they're hungry, a bath when they're dirty, a hug when they fall and hurt themselves. You continue to depend on your family, but in different ways. You can make yourself a snack and take a bath, but you still need guidance and love as you mature and make decisions about your life.

Your interests are also changing, and this affects your relationships. A hobby or activity that you used to share with a friend may no longer be important to you. You might find that you spend less time with that friend, and that your relationship is more superficial. You develop new interests and new friendships.

"Do you want to come over to my house after school?"

"I can't, I'm meeting some other guys."

Adolescence is a time in your life when you begin to assume new responsibilities, and other people's expectations of you change. For example, you agree to mow a neighbour's lawn while she's away. You forget, and when she returns she tells you that she'll find someone else to do it next time. When you were younger, people were more inclined to overlook this kind of forgetfulness. Or maybe your mother or father would have reminded you.

New responsibilities and expectations give you the opportunity to become more independent and reliable. But you may also feel that your relationships with adults are not as comfortable as they were. Parents, teachers, and other adults in your life may seem more critical of you. In turn, you begin to notice that they are not perfect, that they have faults and weaknesses. This experience is a part of growing up.

Changing relationships always involve some stress, but they also provide an opportunity to grow and to learn. The development of deeper, more mature relationships with family members and friends is a special challenge during adolescence. Since each person is unique, no one can predict exactly how well or how easily this challenge will be met. But it is sure that this challenge cannot be avoided. It too is part of growing up.

The Family

From the moment of birth until maturity is a long period of time for human beings. Each person arrives in this world completely helpless and defenceless. The developing individual has many needs — physical, spiritual, emotional, social, intellectual — and these needs are best met within a family. Above all, it is within the family that each person first learns to live in relationship with others.

Living in a Family

Although it is the responsibility of all families to nurture their children, each family is also unique. Each of us grows up in a family, but our experience is not exactly like anyone else's.

• Mai is growing up in an *extended* family. Her family members include her two brothers, her parents, her grandmother, an aunt and uncle, and two cousins. This household of ten people is a busy place, and Mai has never had the experience of coming home to an empty house. Her grandmother manages the house and looks after the children while her parents, aunt, and uncle work.

• Tracey, like many of her friends, is growing up in a *nuclear* family. A nuclear family is one that is limited to parents and children. Her family members include her mother, father, sister, and brother. Some of her extended family members live in the same city, but they do not share her home.

• Tina's family members include her mother, father, and a brother, but several years ago her parents separated and her father and brother now live in another city. Tina lives with her mother, and is growing up in a *single-parent* family. Most single-parent families are headed by women.

• Mark is growing up in a *blended* family. When he was ten years old, his father died. Several years later, his mother married a man who had two boys of his own. It takes a lot of love and patience for people from two different families to become a family.

• Bill is growing up in a *foster* family. His foster parents have three children of their own, and four foster children. Bill lived with his birth mother until he was five. Their life was hard and when it became clear that she was unable to care for him, he came to live with his foster parents. It was a hard time for Bill, since he missed his mother very much. He still sees her occasionally, or talks to her on the telephone. His foster home is a happy one where he has found love and security.

The type of family in which we grow up influences our understanding of what it means to live in a family. For example, Mai's experience is quite different from Tina's. Mai is always surrounded by people, and a large number of adults assume the responsibility of caring for her. Tina and her mother have only each other to depend on. This has made them very close, but there are times when they feel isolated.

Even within a family, each person's experience is different. Brothers and sisters have the same parents and live in the same home, but their family environment is not identical. One important difference is their birth order.

Birth order is the term that is used for children's position in a family — oldest, middle, youngest, only child. Psychologists who study birth order have described some of its effects:

• Parents often have very high expectations for their first child. They expect her or him to be mature, to do well in school, and to take responsibility for younger brothers and sisters. Most firstborn children try to meet their parents' expectations, and so they tend to be good students and to work hard at everything they do. They expect a lot of themselves and worry when they're not successful.

• The youngest child in the family is often the most easy-going. By the time he or she joins the family, parents are more relaxed and have a lot of experience in raising children. Youngest children don't usually worry the way oldest children do, and although they complain about being bossed around, they also enjoy the attention that comes with being the "baby."

• The middle child in the family has a difficult position. It's hard to be neither the oldest nor the youngest. Middle children sometimes feel left out and wish people would pay more attention to them. But as they learn to get along with the oldest and the youngest, they often become quite flexible, and develop a gift for relating to a variety of people.

• An only child tends to have many of the characteristics of oldest children, but doesn't have the experience of growing up with younger brothers and sisters. Only children enjoy the undivided attention of their parents, although at times they miss the companionship that comes with being part of a larger family.

When you read these descriptions, it is important to understand that they are not like scientific facts. There are always exceptions — oldest children who don't do well in school, middle children who have never felt left out, and youngest children who are not at all easy-going. The descriptions provide only a general picture of the influence of birth order. It may help you to understand yourself, your family, and your friends a little bit better.

Communication in the Family

You have been living in your family for a long time, and have had many family experiences. Some of these are special, like a birthday, but most experiences are everyday events — eating meals, getting ready for school, helping at home.

As these everyday experiences are happening, you and your family members are busy communicating with each other.

Day in and day out, family members send messages to each other with their words, tone of voice, the expressions on their faces, gestures, and even with their whole bodies. These messages have to be received and understood. It sounds easy, but you probably know from your own experience that there are times when people don't communicate very well.

Good communication in the family is extremely important. Without it, we cannot share our thoughts and feelings or resolve the normal conflicts that are part of living in a family. When we communicate in a way that is honest, open, and respectful, we are nourishing our family relationships. When we never talk about the things that really matter to us, or are dishonest and disrespectful in the way we communicate, we are hurting these important relationships.

Some Communication Rules

How can families learn to communicate more honestly and openly? First, they have to think about the way they communicate and decide whether there is room for improvement. Most people do see a need for at least some improvement. They want to be more honest and to avoid hurtful disagreements.

The first rule for good communication is:

- LISTEN WITH YOUR MIND AND HEART, NOT JUST YOUR EARS.

41

Are these people listening to each other?

This mother and daughter can hear each other, but they're not listening. If they really listened to each other their conversation might be different:

"Mom, Teresa's invited me to sleep over. Can I go?"

"This isn't the best time to ask me because I'm upset with you about your room. Could you let Teresa know a little later?"

"I'll tell Teresa I'll call her back."

In order to listen, you have to make an effort to understand the other person's feelings and opinions, not just your own. If the girl and her mother ignore each other's concerns (the messy bedroom and the request to stay overnight at Teresa's house), they are going to have difficulty communicating.

A second important rule for good communication in the family is:

What kind of communication difficulty are these people having?

George and his father are obviously doing something wrong. His dad cares about George's mood, but he doesn't express this concern in a clear or tactful way. George would like some privacy, but he communicates his need in a way that annoys and hurts his father. Then his father responds, but he doesn't say what he really means ("Hey, I feel hurt and angry when you push me away like that.")

Here's a more honest and tactful conversation between George and his father:

"Is there something bothering you? You look upset."

"I don't really want to talk about it right now, Dad."

"That's okay. But if I can help, let me know."

These first two rules for good family communication are simple to understand, but are often hard to follow. Our tendency to be selfish is part of the problem. Also, the way in which we communicate becomes a habit, and habits are difficult to break. Learning new ways to communicate in the family takes motivation and real effort.

This is especially true when disagreements and conflicts, which happen in every family, occur. Conflicts can be resolved peacefully, or they can grow and turn into big arguments. In an argument, people express their feelings and opinions, but they are often more concerned with winning than with the other person's feelings and opinions. Most family arguments break the rules for good communication. People don't listen to each other, they don't always say what they mean, and what they say is rarely tactful.

43

The two communication rules you have already discussed are important in situations of conflict. But here is a third rule that can be helpful, particularly for brothers and sisters.

> • DON'T GET INVOLVED IN AN UNNECESSARY CONFLICT.

You probably know from your own experience that some arguments get started for the silliest reasons. A sister teases a brother, and before you know it, they are having a noisy fight. Then their mother or father gets involved and tries to figure out who's right and who's wrong.

The old saying, "It takes two to have an argument," is a good one. How could this argument have been avoided?

Gary sent his brother, John, an invitation to have a fight and John accepted it. He had other choices. He could have ignored Gary's remark completely. Or he could have said, "I really don't like it when you call me stupid, and no, I didn't hear you call me for dinner." Gary might have responded with another insult ("I call you stupid because that's what you are"),

but John would still have a choice about getting into a full–scale battle. Teasing and insults are invitations to an argument or fight and do not have to be accepted.

Earlier we talked about the family as a social environment and its deep influence on each person. Disagreements among family members are a normal part of living in a family.

At times, however, these small conflicts may turn into larger ones. The family environment can become stressful and unhappy. Each person needs to stop and think:

Each family member shares in the responsibility of creating a family environment that is peaceful, open, honest, tactful, and respectful.

Special Issues in Family Living

We have already discussed one issue in family living — communication. As children grow up, there are changes that occur in the family that raise new issues. An issue in family living is anything that is important to family members, and that has an effect on their relationship. An issue is not necessarily a problem, but it is often something that could turn into a problem.

The changes that occur in families as children grow up can be stressful for everyone. Both parents and children have to learn new ways of relating to each other. Some families find this very difficult and certain issues may develop into big problems. Understanding what is happening is helpful, but some stress is unavoidable.

Moods

Living in a family brings people into very close contact with each other. They cannot ignore each other, even if they want to. Family members are usually very aware of each other, and in particular of each other's moods. If one member of the family is sad, upset, or angry, it affects the other members.

Early adolescence is a period of time when some young people experience fluctuating moods. Their moods change very rapidly and the feelings may be quite strong. If this has been happening to you, you have probably found it confusing because there doesn't seem to be an explanation for the way you feel. You wake up in a bad mood and you don't know why. Later on, you feel on top of the world, and you still don't know why. In fact, there is a reason for these changing moods. During puberty the hormone levels in the bloodstream are quite unstable, and this in turn affects the way you feel.

Parents also find adolescents' fluctuating moods confusing. They're not sure how to act. It's difficult to know how to relate to someone who was in a terrible mood in the morning but arrives home after school feeling great.

Moods become an issue in family living if they begin to have a negative effect on family relationships. In order to avoid this, it takes patience and understanding from parents and children. But the person with the biggest responsibility for solving the problem is the one with the bad mood. We are not responsible for feeling depressed or irritable, but we are responsible for managing and controlling these feelings. When moods control us, then we have no choices. We have to yell at people, or be rude to them, or refuse to talk to them.

But when we control our moods and manage our feelings, we have the freedom to:
- avoid getting into discussions that might lead to arguments until the mood passes
- go for a walk, pray, read a good book, watch an interesting television program
- listen to music, draw a picture, get involved in a favourite hobby
- ride a bike, shoot baskets, or go for a fast run
- explain the way we are feeling to our parents and other family members
- apologize when we hurt family members because of our moods.

Moods and Depression

Usually unhappy moods come and go pretty quickly. But sometimes they don't. There might be a reason for a bad mood that lasts — trouble at home or a big argument with a close friend. Or sometimes young people don't know why they feel down, and they can't seem to get out of it. They might have trouble sleeping, lose their appetite, or find it very difficult to concentrate. When people are unhappy day after day, we use the word *depressed* to describe the way they are feeling. As doctors learn more about this condition, they are discovering that some depression may have a physical cause, and can be successfully treated with medication.

When young people are depressed it's very important for them to tell an adult whom they trust about their feelings. In many cases, this person will be one of their parents. Sometimes just talking about unhappy feelings can be helpful. There are other times, however, when the adult may think that the young person should talk to a doctor or a trained counselor, and will help him or her find such a person.

Privacy

Family members like to spend time together, but they also enjoy having privacy. To some degree, this depends on personality. Some people need more privacy than others. But this need always has to be balanced with the need for family intimacy.

Young children don't consider privacy important. They usually prefer to be with other people and they enjoy talking about what is going on in their lives. As children mature and go through puberty, this begins to change. They discover that there are times when they want to be alone and do not want to talk to their family members about what is going on inside them. This is partly because their thoughts and feelings are more complicated, but it is also because they want to be more independent.

Respect for privacy is an important aspect of family living. Knocking on bedroom doors before entering, allowing people time to be alone, asking permission to borrow something, or letting people talk privately on the telephone are only some of the ways that this respect can be shown. But there are also limitations to privacy within the family. Family members do have to communicate with each other in order to be a family. As children grow up it is especially important for them to let their parents know what is going on in their lives. Too little privacy can cause resentments, but too much privacy can interfere with family living. Each family has to try to find the right balance.

Special Challenges to the Family

Every family experiences some stress. There are days when nothing seems to go right — parents are exhausted, children are unco-operative, and the refrigerator stops working.

But there are some situations that are far more stressful than tired parents, unco-operative children, and a warm refrigerator. Some families face difficult and unexpected changes in their lives. Among these special challenges are:

• Serious Illness

When a person develops a serious illness, it is natural for the family members to respond with many feelings: shock, fear, anger, guilt, sadness, and hopelessness. If a child is ill, he or she is likely to receive a lot of attention, and the other children in the family may feel jealous. If a parent is ill, it can be very frightening for the children because they depend on their parents in so many ways.

Serious illness often changes normal family routines, at least for a time. The children in the family may have to assume new responsibilities. Also, there may be financial difficulties, which only increase the stress for the family.

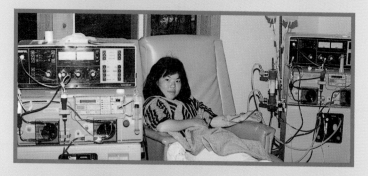

• Unemployment

For many families, even with both parents working, it is a struggle to meet their basic needs. When a parent loses a job, it creates serious stress for the family. There is worry about paying bills, little or no money available for recreation, and the terrible uncertainty of not knowing how long the situation will last. Children find it hard to understand why their parents cannot afford toys, movies, records, or sports equipment. The person who has become unemployed may feel that he or she is a failure.

For families with only one parent, unemployment is a particularly serious problem. Who is going to support the family? Older teen-agers can help, but if they want to remain in school, they have to limit the number of hours they work. Often the only alternative is financial support from the government. This support is one of the ways in which people demonstrate their concern for others. Money that has been collected from those who have jobs (through their taxes) is distributed by the government to help people in need.

• Children with Disabilities

When a child is born with a serious disability, parents are shocked. They may also feel sad, angry, and guilty. Usually they know very little about the particular problem, and so they wonder whether they will be able to cope. Often they receive conflicting advice from doctors, relatives, and friends.

Once the shock has passed, families with disabled children still face special challenges. It may be hard to find the right kind of education for their child. The child may require a great deal of attention, which can mean less time for the other children in the family. Parents of children with serious disabilities also worry about the future. Will the child be able to function as an independent adult? If not, who will provide the care?

Many families meet these special challenges with courage, with hope, and with faith. Family members make a special effort to share their feelings, to be patient with each other, to pray as a family, and to keep a sense of perspective. They are greatly helped by the presence of supportive relatives and friends. The Christian community has an important responsibility to become more aware of special challenges to families, and to respond generously and compassionately.

Family life can be, and for many people is, a joyful experience. Parents find a deep fulfillment as they raise their children, but their role is also a demanding and difficult one. All families have some difficulties. The perfect family doesn't exist, except in our imaginations or on television. Families are never as loving, as patient, and as unselfish as they could be. There are small, daily failures — angry words, a refusal to listen, misunderstandings, unintended injustices. This is why forgiveness is so important among family members.

But there are also times when a family may experience larger failures — lack of acceptance, unwillingness to forgive, a breakdown of the relationship among family members, an emotional environment in which it is difficult for people to grow. No one begins a marriage and family wanting such things to happen. When Pope John Paul II came to Canada in 1984, he spoke to the young people in Montreal about the pain and sadness of family difficulties. This is part of what he said:

"Too many of you suffer because of the breakdown of family life, because of separation and divorce; and you have been wounded to the point of sometimes doubting whether a faithful and lasting love is possible.

It is not ours to judge those who have been hurt by the upheaval affecting morals and society. But I say to you: do not doubt; you can build a home on the rock of fidelity, because you can count totally on the fidelity of God, who is love."

Children and young people who have been hurt in their families need to know that they do not have to grow up bitter and angry, repeating the difficulties of the past. There are signs of God's love in each life, and the discovery of these signs leads to compassion, forgiveness, and hope.

Friendship

"The best mirror is an old friend."
(George Herbert)

"Let kindliness and loyalty never leave you. . ."
(Proverbs)

"A friend is a friend at all times. . ."
(Proverbs)

"A new friend is like new wine; when it has aged you will drink it with pleasure."
(Sirach)

"The only way to have a friend is to be one." (Emerson)

"We are advertised by our loving friends."
(Shakespeare)

"A faithful friend is a sturdy shelter."
(Sirach)

In some ways, each friendship is as unique as the people involved. Some friends share many interests in common; others share very few. In some cases, people with similar personalities are drawn toward each other. But it also happens that two people who are complete opposites are the closest of friends.

But there are certain characteristics that all good friendships have in common. From the list below, which qualities would you choose as absolutely essential for friendship?

- loyal
- easy-going
- loves sports
- interested in me
- attractive

- fun to be with
- makes me feel accepted
- popular
- does well in school

- serious
- lives near me
- sophisticated
- wears the right clothes

I don't know why I hang around with the guy. You should have been there. He made a real jerk of himself.

Danny and Frank have been friends for a number of years. But whenever Frank gets the opportunity, he talks about Danny behind his back. Is this a real friendship?

Loyalty is an essential sign of friendship. You cannot share your feelings, thoughts, and experiences with someone you do not trust. Friends have the right to expect loyalty from each other. If they have a disagreement, they settle it themselves without complaining about each other to other people. It's important, however, not to confuse loyalty with possession. A friend is not disloyal because he or she spends time with another person. Friends have to be free to relate to many different people.

Since friendship is a personal relationship, it involves getting to know the other person. If you have no interest in someone's opinions, talents, problems, feelings, or experiences, then you are not likely to become friends. You may share an activity such as sports or music, but unless you develop a personal interest in each other, the relationship is not likely to deepen.

Carol would like to be friends with Nancy because Nancy is extremely popular with the other girls in the class. Nancy has never shown any interest in Carol. Do they have a basis for friendship?

Jack and Maria have been friends since they were in Grade 1. Lately, Maria is always criticising Jack's behaviour and opinions. What is likely to happen to their friendship? What would you do if you were Jack?

As people become friends, they come to accept and affirm each other. They admire certain qualities in each other, and are tolerant and forgiving of faults and weaknesses. They may have had an argument at home, or a problem with the teacher, but when they're together, things don't look so bad. Acceptance is necessary for friendship.

Without loyalty, personal interest, and acceptance, relationships that may seem like friendships can become exploitive. *Exploitation* means to use people for selfish reasons. One person wants to get something from another person instead of wanting to give something:

- An unpopular person wants to get status by having a relationship with someone who is popular.
- An aggressive person wants to get a feeling of power by having a relationship with someone who is weaker and dependent.

When this happens between people who are supposed to be friends, it harms both of them. Friendship is meant to bring out the best in people — unselfishness, generosity, wanting what is good for another person. Exploitation is really the opposite of friendship.

Sometimes people don't recognize that they are being exploited. Or perhaps they're comfortable with the situation and don't want to change. Or, they may feel trapped, but don't realize that they have the freedom to say no. Talking to another person — a parent, a teacher, or a trusted friend — about the situation can be helpful.

Not all friendships develop into close relationships. Usually people have one or two best friends with whom they can be intimate. As well, they are often part of a larger group of friends who give them a sense of belonging, but with whom their relationship is less intimate. The people in this group enjoy each other's company and often do things together.

Beyond this group, most people also have acquaintance-friends. These are people whom they see regularly, but do not really know very well. Acquaintance-friends might be in the same classroom, belong to the same sports team, or have a shared interest such as music. Best friends, group friends, and acquaintance-friends — each type of relationship is important.

As you develop and discover more about yourself, your relationships will change. New friendships will begin, and others will weaken or come to an end. You might find that you are no longer comfortable with the people in your larger group of friends because their interests or values differ from yours.

Changes in relationships are stressful and people's feelings do get hurt. It is hard to end a friendship, especially when one person does not want it to happen. Usually, however, friendships do not stop suddenly. Instead, people begin to spend less time with each other and gradually drift apart as other relationships become more important. It is also stressful to detach yourself from a group of friends, even if you have good reasons for doing so. You miss the sense of identity and belonging that the group provides. Stress, hurt feelings, worries about friendship — these are difficult, but normal experiences as people learn how to live the relationship of friendship.

Issues in Friendship

At this time in your life your relationships with people your own age are important to you. The experience of being with friends is an enjoyable and necessary part of your development. You learn to relate to many different people, you discover more about yourself, and you clarify your opinions and values as you communicate with your friends. With close friends you also have the opportunity to give and receive acceptance, affirmation, and loyalty. You discover the value of being a friend.

But an intense preoccupation with friendship also raises new issues that need some reflection. A sense of balance in friendship is just as important as it is in family life.

Peer Pressure

The desire to belong and to be accepted is an essential human need. When children are very young this need is met almost entirely by the family. Later, at school, children also look for acceptance and a sense of belonging from their classmates and teachers. They want to be liked, to be approved of, to be a part of the group. But it is not as easy to be accepted at school as it is at home. They can't talk whenever they want, they have to take turns, co-operate, and compromise. Because children want to belong and to be accepted, they develop these relationship skills.

Around your age, and for the next few years, the need to be accepted by your peers is especially strong. This is because you are slowly growing up and beginning to discover who you are, not just as a member of your family, but as a separate person. This has to happen in order for you to become a fully independent adult.

Peer groups, offer you companionship, a sense of belonging, advice, sympathy, and a feeling of independence from your family. But a peer group can also have very strong, unspoken rules for membership. In order to be accepted, these rules have to be followed. This may include the way people dress and wear their hair, their activities, their attitudes toward school and family, their tastes in music and fashion, and the values that they hold.

If the rules of your peer group are in conflict with your beliefs and values or those of your family, the result will be pressure on you. On the one hand, you want to be accepted by the group. On the other hand, you do not want to act against your values. At the very least, you worry about the consequences of ignoring your parents' wishes.

Peer pressure can be positive or negative. If you become part of a group that disapproves of smoking or skipping school, you will feel pressured not to smoke or skip school. If your group of friends believes that it important to do well in school, then chances are that you will also. This kind of peer pressure is positive since it encourages you to develop in the right direction, and is supportive of good habits.

But most often when people talk about peer pressure they mean the negative kind. Negative peer pressure can range from minor issues such as clothing that parents disapprove of to very serious problems involving alcohol and drug abuse, delinquency, and early sexual activity. Most young people believe that they can resist negative peer pressure, and it is undoubtedly true that some of them can. But it can be very difficult for people not to go along with the group when they have a very strong need to belong and to be accepted. This is the main reason why parents worry so much about their children's choice of friends.

Understanding peer pressure will not eliminate it from your life, but it may help you develop ways of handling it. You have many roles in your life and being a friend is only one of them. It is an important role, but it has to be balanced with your other roles — member of a family, student, and developing individual.

Balancing Family and Friends

As children grow up, their friendships sometimes become an issue within families. This is a new tension that happens for several reasons:

- As young people spend more time with friends, they spend less time with their families. This big change for families creates some stress.

- Parents are aware of the strong influence friends have on each other. They want their children to have friends who have healthy attitudes and strong values.
- Since friendship is a relationship that people choose for themselves, young people may resent their parents' concern about their choice of friends.

Because this issue is so important to parents and children, it can easily lead to conflict. This is another situation where communication rules are very important.

When friendship has become a family issue, it can be helpful for parents and children to have a discussion about it at a time when they are relaxed and getting along with each other. What is most important is that they listen to each other's point of view and communicate in an honest and respectful manner. When people aren't listening to each other, they often exaggerate and say things like, "You hate all my friends!" or "You never spend any time at home!" These kinds of messages are invitations to an argument, not a discussion.

There are many compromises that parents and children can work out, for example:

• Parents could agree to stop criticizing their children's friends. If they have a serious concern, however, they have the responsibility to communicate it honestly and respectfully.

• Children could agree to spend more time with the family and to a specific limit on the amount of time they spend on the telephone.

• Parents and children could plan family activities that appeal to older children and could, at times, include friends.

Each family will have its own way of handling this issue. Some families will expect children to spend more time at home than others. In one family the issue of balancing friendship and family may lead to a lot of conflict and unhappiness. In another family, it may not even be an issue. But in all families there is a need for balance. Family relationships are irreplaceable, and need attention to remain healthy. Friendship relationships are also precious and should never be neglected. Both kinds of relationships are essential in the life of each person.

"You mean your friend's parents allow him to dress that way?"

"You're spending an awful lot of time with Lisa. What happened to that nice girl, Susan? Aren't you friends any more?".

"Yes, we expect you to come with us to your grandmother's."

To be a person is to live in relationship with others. We depend on our relationships; without them, we could not thrive. Our family members, who first offer us love, acceptance, trust, and forgiveness, give us the confidence and the generosity to offer the gift of friendship and intimacy to others.

Our social nature also draws us toward group activities. Teams, clubs, bands, choirs, after-school programs, community activities — these groups offer us the opportunity to relax, play a game, exercise, pursue an interest, or create music. But we participate in these activities not just as individuals, but as members of a group. We relate to the other people in the group in a special way. Together, we are accomplishing something that we could not accomplish alone. We enjoy the activity as an individual, but we also appreciate what the whole group accomplishes.

We have many different relationships, and each one is valuable. Not all of them are intimate, and this is as it should be. But all of our relationships can be friendly and respectful whether we are buying a candy bar from someone, saying hello to a neighbour, or sharing a seat on the school bus.

Human relationships always have the potential to cause pain. This is because they are so important to us. But they also have the potential to bring great joy. Both the pain and the joy are part of each person's experience. They cannot be avoided if we are to be fully human.

Great Things Have Happened

We were talking about the great things
that have happened in our lifetimes;
and I said, "Oh, I suppose the moon landing
was the greatest thing that has happened
in my time." But, of course, we were all lying.
The truth is the moon landing didn't mean
one-tenth as much to me as one night in 1963
when we lived in a three-room flat in what once
   had been
the mansion of some Victorian merchant prince
(our kitchen had been a clothes closet, I'm sure),
on a street where by now nobody lived
who could afford to live anywhere else.
That night, the three of us, Claudine, Johnnie and me,
woke up at half-past four in the morning
and ate cinnamon toast together.

   "Is that all?" I hear somebody ask.

Oh, but we were silly with sleepiness
and, under our windows, the street-cleaners
were working their machines and conversing in
   Italian, and
everything was strange without being threatening,
even the tea-kettle whistled differently
than in the daytime: it was like the feeling
you get sometimes in a country you've never visited
before, when the bread doesn't taste quite the same,
the butter is a small adventure, and they put
paprika on the table instead of pepper,
except that there was nobody in this country
except the three of us, half-tipsy with the wonder
of being alive, and wholly enveloped in love.

Alden Nowlan

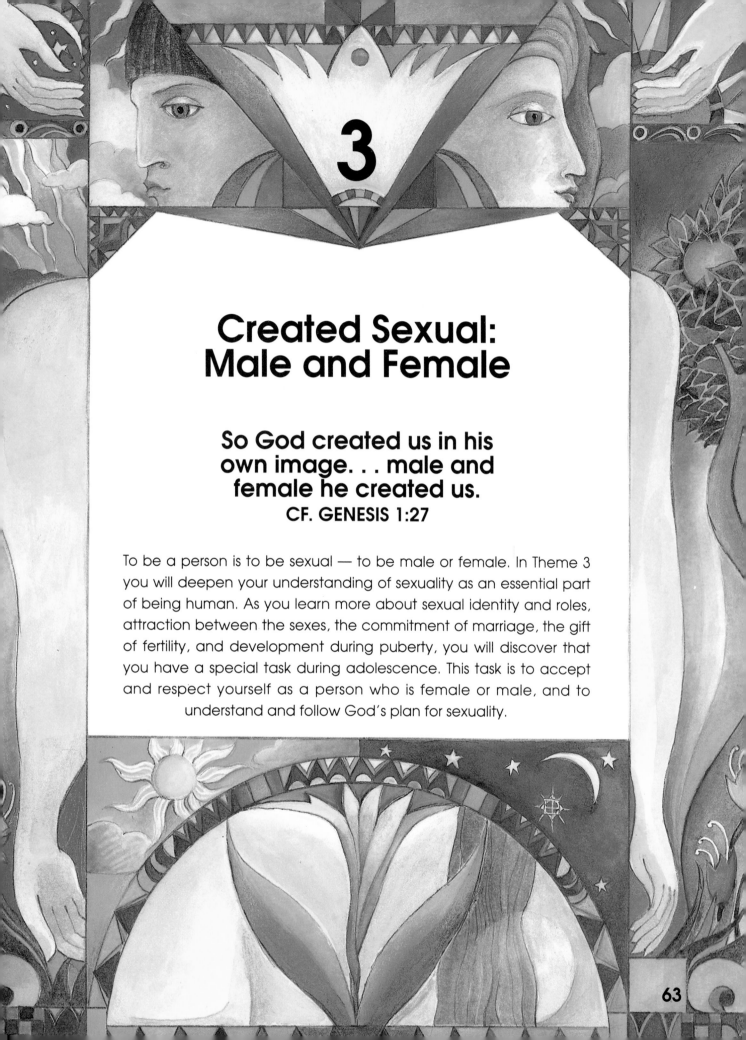

Created Sexual: Male and Female

So God created us in his own image. . . male and female he created us.
CF. GENESIS 1:27

To be a person is to be sexual — to be male or female. In Theme 3 you will deepen your understanding of sexuality as an essential part of being human. As you learn more about sexual identity and roles, attraction between the sexes, the commitment of marriage, the gift of fertility, and development during puberty, you will discover that you have a special task during adolescence. This task is to accept and respect yourself as a person who is female or male, and to understand and follow God's plan for sexuality.

What is Sexuality?

Sexuality is expressed in and through our bodies, feelings, thoughts, attitudes, personalities, beliefs, and values.

What does it mean to be a person? Why are human relationships so important? How do we learn to live in relationship with others?

These are some of the personal and complex questions we have been exploring. Now we turn to another question about the human person — what is sexuality? It too is a question that is intensely personal and complex.

Each human person is created sexual. We are either male or female. We live in relationship with other people as sexual persons. Our sexuality, like our personality, is not something that we have; it is something that we are.

Sexuality is not the same thing as sex, sexual characteristics, sexual identity, or sexual roles. These are all aspects of sexuality, but they are only part of the picture.

• **Sex**, or gender, is determined by the sex chromosome from the father (X or Y) and the sex chromosome from the mother (X). Unlike the other major body systems, the reproductive systems of males and females are different. A baby girl will have female external and internal reproductive organs, while a baby boy will have male external and internal reproductive organs.

• **The sexual characteristics** of adult males and females are obviously different. In young children, these differences are apparent only in the external genitals. At puberty, male and female secondary sexual characteristics begin to develop and the differences between the sexes become apparent in the entire body.

• **Sexual identity** is a person's understanding of herself as a female, or of himself as a male. Children first begin to have a sense of sexual identity when they are around two years old.

• **Sexual roles** refer to the way males and females are expected to act in a particular society. Depending on the society, sexual roles can be rigid or flexible. People learn about sexual roles from their families, friends, parish, members of various groups to which they belong, and media.

The full meaning of sexuality can only be discovered in the meaning of the human person. It is not just the body that is sexual; it is the whole person, the body-spirit, who is sexual. When a girl or woman describes herself, she says, "I *am* female," not, "I have a female body." In the same way, the boy or man *is* male, not someone who has a male body.

Understanding Sexuality

We express ourselves as males and females in different ways at different times in our lives. When children are very young they learn to relate to family members and friends. They form attachments to people and learn how to express these attachments. Gestures of affection, playing with friends, showing interest in other people, co-operation — these are all ways in which growing children express who they are as boys and girls with their family members and friends.

At puberty we begin to discover a new dimension to our relationships. As the body matures and becomes more adult, a strong physical attraction between males and females usually develops. Sexual attraction is a new experience that takes time to understand and to learn how to fit into our relationships.

With maturity, sexual attraction can grow into a deep, personal relationship between a man and a woman that leads to marriage. In marriage, a husband and wife give themselves to each other in total and intimate friendship. Sexual intercourse is a special expression of this gift. Without words, a husband and wife say to each other:

• I give myself to you, I accept you, I love you, I trust you, I will always be faithful to you, I will always forgive you, I accept whatever the future holds for us.

Acceptance of what the future holds includes the gift of fertility. Human fertility, which is the power to give life, is an essential part of sexuality. The first signs of fertility are experienced at puberty when the reproductive systems of males and females begin to mature. Like sexual attraction, this is a new experience for males and females that takes time to understand and accept. They have to become familiar with their changing bodies, and with the signs of their fertility.

The deeply committed relationship of marriage is the foundation on which a family is built. This is why the life-giving power of fertility is intended to be used only in marriage. In sexual intercourse, a husband and wife communicate not only their love, commitment, and sense of belonging, but also their willingness to accept the gift of fertility and their openness to the new human life that may be the result of their love.

You have, of course, been learning about sexuality since the day you were born. Your family members, your friends, and many other people have taught you a great deal about being male or female. Through your relationships, you have discovered how wonderful it is to be accepted, loved, and trusted; and you have learned to offer the gift of acceptance, love, and trust to others. Now you have a new task ahead of you: to learn how to integrate your developing sexuality into your life, and to live in harmony with it.

Sexual Identity and Sexual Roles

Children usually take their sexual identity for granted. They don't spend much time thinking about it and they tend to be more involved with their own sex than with the opposite sex. This attitude begins to change in early adolescence. Some young people suddenly become very aware of themselves as males and females, curious about each other, and interested in relationships with the opposite sex. For others, their attitude changes very slowly over a number of years. This second group of young people sometimes wonder what all the fuss is about. They don't spend a lot of time daydreaming about being grown up, thinking about their masculinity or femininity, or worrying about whether they are attractive.

Both attitudes are completely normal. Just as physical development during puberty begins at different times and can be fast or slow, an interest in sexual identity, sexual roles, and relationships with the opposite sex can begin early or late in adolescence, and may develop quickly or slowly over a number of years.

Most children know which sex they are by the time they are two, or sometimes even younger.

Growing Up as Males and Females

Our understanding of ourselves as males and females is called *sexual identity*. Sexual identity includes knowing which sex you are (*gender identity*) and your ideas about the way males and females are expected to act in a particular society (*sexual roles*).

From the time they are born, children begin to learn about sexual roles. Sexual roles include standards not only for behaviour, but also for appearance, personality traits, interests, and careers. Children learn about the way males and females are supposed to act from their families, their friends, and from the books they read and the television programs they watch.

What do these scenes tell you about children's understanding of sexual roles?

When three-year-olds play house, they have no trouble figuring out who should be the mother and who should be the father. But these two children, Jenny and Martin, ran into a problem because they have each learned something different about sexual roles. In Jenny's family, her mother always cooks dinner. In Martin's family, sometimes his father cooks, and sometimes his mother cooks. No one ever told Jenny that only women could cook dinner, but this is what she has picked up from living in her family. Since young children's ideas about sexual roles tend to be quite rigid, if they have never seen a man cooking, they tend to believe that it's impossible.

Girls

Girls are nicer than boys.

Boys fight all the time and girls don't.

It's more fun to play with girls because boys are rough and mean.

Girls are smarter than boys.

Boys

Boys are more fun than girls.

Girls are silly, and they always tell on you.

Boys are stronger than girls.

Boys get into trouble more than girls.

A grade three teacher asked her students this question: What do you think are the differences between boys and girls?

These answers tell you something very important about developing girls and boys. They usually prefer their own sex, and they often have less than positive views about the opposite sex. Some psychologists suspect that this may be a necessary stage as children develop a sense of sexual identity. They aren't mature enough to realize that when they value their own sex, they don't have to devalue the opposite sex. The fact that in any grade three classroom there are boys who don't enjoy fighting, girls who never tattle, boys who aren't particularly strong, and girls who enjoy rough play doesn't seem to be relevant. Instead of noticing all the differences among the boys and girls they know, they tend to think in stereotypes — a positive stereotype for their own sex, and a somewhat negative one for the opposite sex. It is not until children are a few years older that their ideas about the differences between males and females become more flexible.

The changes of puberty focus young people's attention on sexual identity. Instead of taking it for granted as children do, they become more aware of it, and they have new questions about sexual roles. What does it mean to be female and behave in a feminine way, to be male and behave in a masculine way? Do I measure up as a female or as a male?

Femininity and masculinity are the behaviours, interests, and qualities that are associated with being female and male. You did not develop your ideas about masculinity and femininity by yourself. Your family, your teachers, your classmates, your friends, your faith community, and the media have had an important influence on your ideas — about how you should look and behave, what are appropriate interests for your sex, what personality traits are valued in your sex, and what kind of aspirations you should have for your future.

Indirectly or directly, they have provided you with a set of criteria for masculinity and femininity. *Criteria* are standards for judging or criticising something. Your task during adolescence is to become aware of these criteria, and to examine them. You may decide to keep some and to reject others, and as you continue to grow, you will also discover new ones. By the time you are an adult, you will want to be sure that your criteria for masculinity and femininity are truly your own, and are in keeping with Christian values.

What do you think of these criteria for masculinity and femininity?

Males are not supposed to cry.

It is important for females to have careers.

Males find fatherhood very enjoyable.

Females with well-developed bodies are sexy.

71

Your criteria for femininity and masculinity are also influenced by people who serve as role models for you. You observe their appearance and behaviour, notice their interests and personality traits, and listen to them talk about their hopes, or about the work they do. Some of your role models are famous people you have never met. Others you see everyday. You may admire certain people so much that you dress the way they do, or imitate their mannerisms. This is all part of growing up and learning more about being male and female. You will explore many aspects of maleness and femaleness during your adolescence. But you will want to be careful that you don't lose sight of yourself and the value of being the unique person that you are.

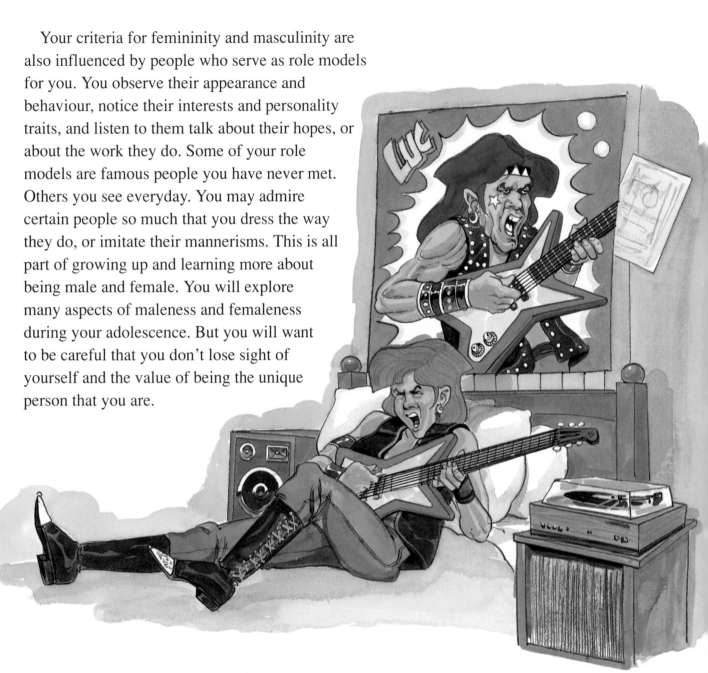

Understanding Sexual Roles

As you learn more about your sexual identity and explore different views about sexual roles, it is important to be aware of sexual stereotypes. A stereotype is a belief about a particular group of people that is overly simple, often incorrect, and is applied to every member of the group. Stereotypes about any group of individuals — men, women, the elderly, teen-agers, or people of different races — ignore the uniqueness of people. People are far too complex and mysterious to be summed up by a stereotype.

Sexual stereotypes often exaggerate the differences between the sexes, and can result in limiting the activities and experiences of both sexes. It is unfortunate when people limit themselves and their understanding of the opposite sex to a narrow and rigid set of criteria or stereotypes. It can also lead to injustice. Each group, males and females, is made up of unique individuals who need to grow, to develop their interests and personalities, to plan their futures, and to learn to live in friendship with one another.

It is not easy to sort out all of the ideas you have absorbed about maleness and femaleness. You will probably discover that some of your criteria conflict. For example, in your family you may have learned that males and females should develop their interests, whatever these may be. But what if you belong to a group of friends that doesn't share these flexible views about male and female interests? Whose criteria will you follow?

Tom has this problem. He is an avid reader, and he also loves classical music. His friends do not share his interests. They are very keen on sports and popular music. Will Tom hide or drop the interests that are important to him because they are not valued by his peer group? If he doesn't share the interests that are valued by the boys in his group, does that make him less masculine?

It is important to remember that there are important cultural differences within our society in the way people understand sexual roles. These differences are especially obvious in the way families are organized.

In some families, the roles of men and women are quite distinct. Women are responsible for caring for the children and for most of the work in the home. Men have outside jobs and support the family. Even when women also have jobs outside the home, these distinctions remain. Expectations for children are also distinguished acccording to sex. Girls are expected to help their mothers with tasks like cooking and cleaning. Boys help their fathers with tasks like household repairs, shoveling snow, or taking out garbage.

In other families, the roles of men and women overlap to a much greater degree. The tasks of supporting the family, of raising children, and of caring for the home are shared by both sexes. Children are expected to help, but chores are not assigned according to sex. Boys can help with cooking, and girls can paint, mow the lawn, and take out the garbage.

Your family may be something like one of these two types of families, or it may be somewhere in between. Or you may be living with one parent who has all of the responsibilities for your family.

No matter how sexual roles are defined, it is essential that both male and female roles are valued and that the work of each sex within the family, and outside the family is respected. Men and women are intended to complement each other. This means they are intended to develop their personal gifts, and to share them with each other. They are meant to be help-mates.

The Human Body

There are two periods in our lives when the human body changes very rapidly and quite dramatically. The first period went by without your noticing it, but the adults around you were very aware of the changes in your body. In the first year of your life you probably tripled your birth weight, and by the time you were about two and a half years old, you had already reached half of your adult height. Imagine how large you would be now had you continued growing at that rate!

The second period of rapid growth and significant body change occurs at puberty. The shape of the body changes, there are obvious signs of the development of fertility, and a growth spurt results in a rapid change in height and weight. Even the appearance of the face is changed because of the growth of the facial bones.

These important changes lead to an increase in awareness of the body. At some time or another, young people who are going through puberty become very conscious of their bodies and concerned about their appearance. They may feel awkward because they aren't used to their new height and shape, or self-conscious because they are growing faster or slower than their friends. These are natural responses to such big changes.

76

Body Image During Puberty

Part of each person's self-concept is something we call a *body image*. Your body image is your concept or idea of how your body is put together, and what your appearance is like. A body image can be positive or negative, accurate or distorted. Most people have a reasonably accurate body image, but they are likely to be dissatisfied with some aspects of their appearance. One person doesn't like his nose. Another wishes she were taller. These small dissatisfactions are a normal human experience. But part of self-acceptance is learning to develop a positive attitude toward your body, and not taking your dissatisfactions too seriously.

Tracey is unhappy with some aspects of her appearance. She thinks she's too large, and her face looks strange to her. Almost every morning she and her brother have a conversation like this one.

Adolescents often get teased about the amount of time they spend looking in the mirror. But it takes time to become comfortable with a new appearance, and examining your reflection is one of the ways you do it. When young adolescents look in the mirror, however, they tend to exaggerate their small imperfections. As a result, they may develop a negative body image. This in turn can have an effect on their self-concept. There are several reasons why this happens:

• During adolescence people often spend a lot of time thinking about their appearance. This is normal, but whenever attention is turned inward instead of outward toward others, inadequacies and weaknesses tend to be highlighted instead of gifts and strengths. Too often, people are inclined to see ugliness in themselves instead of beauty. That is why the experience of being accepted and loved is so essential. Others see our gifts and strengths and help us to turn our attention away from ourselves and our inadequacies.

• Adolescence is a time when being accepted is very important. Everyone wants to belong, to fit in with the group. But the physical changes of puberty happen at different times and at different rates. Adolescents are often unhappy with their appearance because they have not yet begun to develop, or because they are much more developed than most of the people around them.

• Media, and especially advertising, influence body images. Certain standards are set for what is considered attractive. For example, females must be very thin, or wear their hair in a particular way. Males must be tall and muscular. We look at these images and they become part of us, often without much thought on our part. We measure ourselves against these unrealistic standards of attractiveness, and become dissatisfied. The more uncertain people are about their appearance or their attractiveness, the more influenced they will be by these images. Since it is natural to be somewhat uncertain about the body during puberty, media images often have a strong influence at this time and may contribute to a negative body image.

Understanding why people can develop a negative body image during puberty does not prevent it from occurring, but can help keep it in perspective. Physical appearance is only one aspect of self-concept. It's important not to let it take over your whole life.

Even though adolescents often worry about their appearance, they don't always give their bodies the basic care that is needed. Adequate rest and nourishing food are especially important at this time. It's easier to withstand the ups and downs of adolescence when you are well-fed and well-rested. Regular physical exercise is also important. Many young people have a tendency to become much less active during adolescence. This is unfortunate because exercise is necessary for the physical

health of the body, has a positive effect on people's moods, and contributes to an attractive appearance.

Caring for the body also includes personal hygiene, which becomes more important during puberty. As the sweat glands develop, the body perspires more, and this perspiration has a stronger odour. The glands beneath the skin also begin to produce more oil, affecting skin and hair. As a result, frequent showers or baths are much more essential than they were during childhood.

Health and Body Image

Weight is often a big issue for adolescent girls, and indeed for many adult women. It is normal for females to have more body fat than males. In fact, without a certain percentage of body fat, menstruation cannot occur.

When girls experience the rapid weight gain of puberty, they may become concerned, especially when they do not have the long thin body that they see in so many fashion magazines. For some girls, their dissatisfaction with their bodies leads them to diet so severely that they harm their health and even stunt their growth. Adolescence is a time when a healthy diet is especially important because of rapid bone growth.

Unfortunately, for a few teen-agers, a preoccupation with weight and dieting can contribute to the development of a serious eating disorder such as *anorexia nervosa* (dieting to the point of near starvation) or *bulimia* (eating very large amounts of foods and then getting rid of it by vomiting or taking a lot of laxatives). Both of these eating disorders are dangerous, are almost exclusively experienced by females, and require specialized medical treatment.

A Growing Awareness of Fertility

The most significant physical change that takes place during puberty is the development of the capacity to reproduce. But this physical change is not obvious in the way that the external changes in the body are. There are definite signs when fertility is developing in males and females, but these signs are experienced privately. When young people do not understand what is happening to their bodies, they may feel confused or overwhelmed. They may wonder if they are normal. By learning to recognize and understand the signs of fertility, they become more comfortable with their bodies and with the experience of puberty.

Female Fertility

Many natural events occur in cycles. For example, in our climate the four seasons follow one another year after year. A *cycle* is a series of events with a beginning and an ending, which are repeated again and again in the same order. The word *cycle* is often used to describe female fertility.

A female fertility cycle is the time between the beginning of one period of menstruation and the beginning of the next period of menstruation. Most cycles last from three to five weeks and include a short period of fertility and a longer period of infertility. In other words, women are fertile only at a certain time during their cycles. In contrast, men are continuously fertile.

Female Fertility Cycle

Cycles vary from woman to woman and each woman's cycle also varies. A thirty day cycle could look like this.

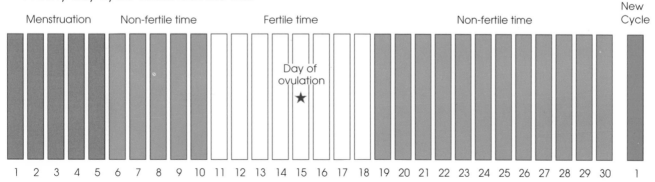

Menstruation   Non-fertile time   Fertile time   Non-fertile time   New Cycle

Day of ovulation ★

1 2 3 4 5 6 7 8 9 10 11 12 13 14 15 16 17 18 19 20 21 22 23 24 25 26 27 28 29 30   1

Regular events that occur during the adult female cycle are:

• **Menstruation**, which is usually referred to as the beginning of the cycle. The lining of the uterus, which has developed in preparation for receiving a new life, is made up of cells and tiny blood vessels. When fertilization does not take place, this lining disintegrates and flows out of the body through the vagina. It normally takes from two to seven days for menstruation to be completed, and this process is often called a *period*.

• A time of rest before an ovum begins to ripen. This time of rest may occur in some cycles and not in others.

• The **ripening of an ovum** in the ovaries. Before a girl is born, her two ovaries already contain ova (egg cells), but these cells are immature. The ova are surrounded by other cells, and together a group of cells and an immature ovum are called a *follicle*. During an adult woman's cycle the follicle grows and the ovum matures. Meanwhile, the lining of the uterus is again rebuilding in preparation for a new life.

• **Ovulation**, which occurs when the ovum is fully ripened. The ovum leaves the follicle and moves into the fallopian tube, which leads to the uterus. The period of time just before and immediately after ovulation is the fertile time in a woman's cycle.

If there is no pregnancy, approximately two weeks after ovulation, the lining of the uterus begins to disintegrate so that a new lining can develop. Menstruation occurs and the cycle begins again.

Menstruation is the most obvious sign of the female fertility cycle, but not the only one. As an ovum begins to ripen in the follicle, the ovaries send a signal to the cervix, the opening at the bottom of the uterus, to produce mucus. At first this cervical mucus is quite thick, but gradually, as ovulation approaches, it becomes thinner, more transparent, and elastic. After ovulation, the mucus thickens again and forms a barrier or plug at the opening of the uterus. In this way the opening to the uterus is sealed in order to protect the reproductive system from infection. The mucus plug also offers protection to a new life that might be growing inside the uterus.

Cervical mucus is a sign of female fertility. As it becomes thinner, women become aware of it outside the vagina. Later in their cycle, they are likely to notice that the mucus has disappeared. The purpose of the cervical mucus is to:
- nourish and prolong the life of the sperm cells
- guide and carry sperm toward the ovum
- filter out abnormal or immature sperm cells.

Sometime after girls begin to mature, they experience these signs of their fertility. Menstruation, which first happens when girls are between nine and sixteen years old, is a sign that the uterus has begun its task of building a lining. But it may be several years before menstruation occurs regularly. The hormone levels that are necessary to build a lining in the uterus are not yet stable in young girls. For this reason, it can be several months or even longer between periods of menstruation.

When girls first begin to mature, they may not notice the presence of cervical mucus, or they may misinterpret it. Sometimes they think that there is something wrong with them. But the appearance of mucus during their cycle is a natural sign of female fertility, indicating that ovulation is occurring. Young girls, however, do not always ovulate every cycle even though they are menstruating. The hormones that stimulate ovulation may not always reach a high enough level. By the time girls are in their late teens, however, they are usually ovulating during each cycle.

Male Fertility

Male fertility, unlike female fertility, does not occur in a cycle. Once males are past puberty, their fertility is continuous. Physically mature males always have the ability to reproduce. Of course, like any other system of the body, both male and female fertility can be impaired by health problems.

Fertility begins in males with the production of sperm cells. This process usually starts when boys are between twelve and sixteen years of age. Sperm are first formed in tiny tubes inside the testicles. As the sperm mature, they travel to a larger tube, which is called the *vas deferens*. There are two of these larger tubes, one for each testicle.

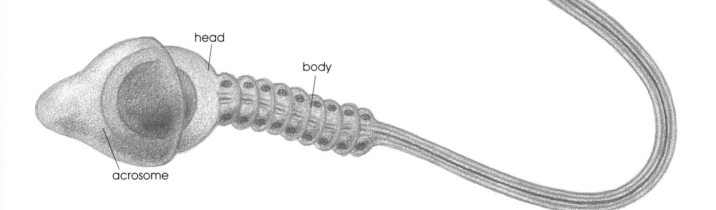

tail

head

body

acrosome

The head of the sperm contains the genetic material. It is covered by the acrosome, which contains enzmes that allow the sperm to penetrate the ovum. The body provides energy for movement, and the tail moves the sperm forward.

Sometimes boys wonder why the testicles are on the outside of the body where they are vulnerable to injury. The reason is that sperm production requires a temperature that is slightly cooler than the rest of the body. The scrotum, which is the sac of skin covering the testicles, actually regulates the temperature of the testicles. It does this by contracting and pulling the testicles closer to the body when more warmth is needed, or by relaxing and allowing the testicles to move away from the body when a cooler temperature is needed.

In order to leave the body, sperm cells must move out of the storage areas and mix with several fluids, which protect and nourish the sperm. The mixture of sperm and nourishing fluids is called *semen*. Semen is expelled from the body through the penis by a process that is called *ejaculation*. Ejaculation is caused by a series of contractions within the man's body that force the semen through the urethra, and out the end of the penis. The amount of semen that is expelled is very small, but it may contain several hundred million sperm cells.

In order for ejaculation to take place, the man must experience an *erection*. An erection occurs when there is an increase in blood flow to the penis. As the tissues in the penis are filled with blood, the penis becomes larger and rigid. This physical change makes it possible for the man's penis to enter a woman's vagina during sexual intercourse. Ejaculation cannot occur without an erection, but an erection is not always followed by ejaculation.

Even baby boys experience erections, but it is not until after puberty that ejaculations can occur. Sometime after sperm production has begun inside the testicles, boys ejaculate for the first time. This occurs because only a limited amount of sperm can be stored inside the body. In order to make room for new sperm cells, semen is cleared out of the body periodically. This can happen gradually, but usually it happens all at once through an ejaculation. Often this clearing out process occurs while boys are sleeping, and so it is called a *nocturnal emission* or *wet dream*. Nocturnal emissions are an important sign of male fertility. The boy has begun to produce life-giving cells.

The Stages of Puberty

The beginning of puberty is set in motion by the *endocrine glands*. These glands secrete chemical substances called *hormones*. As hormones move through the blood, they act like messengers, telling various systems in the body what to do.

Earlier, we talked about moods and the effect that hormones have on them. During puberty, the hormone levels in the blood can be quite unstable. At one time they may be very high, at another, quite low. This has an effect on people's emotions, and on the way they react to events and to other people. Like the hormone levels, moods tend to swing during puberty between highs and lows. As development progresses and the body matures, hormone production becomes more stable, and moods level out.

The activity of your endocrine glands occurs automatically within your body. Puberty begins at different times for different people, but once started, development will occur. It may take one person longer to develop than another, but the same level of sexual maturation is eventually achieved.

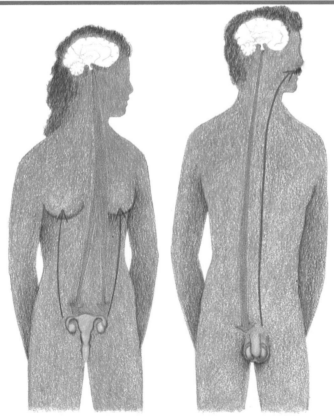

Growth and sexual development are controlled by the endocrine glands. One of these glands is located at the base of the brain and is called the pituitary gland. Although very tiny, the pituitary gland is responsible for the beginning of puberty by releasing two types of hormones into the blood stream. The first type stimulates general growth; the second type acts directly on the male and female reproductive systems and stimulates the maturation of ova and the production of sperm cells. These hormones also act as messengers to the ovaries and testicles, telling them to produce other hormones that are necessary for reproduction. The ovaries begin to secrete estrogen and progesterone, and the testicles begin to produce testosterone. These hormones are essential for male and female fertility, and for the development of the secondary sexual characteristics.

Very few changes in our lives happen all at once. Whether it is the kind of change that takes place when we learn a new skill or a change in the body, it takes time and many small steps before the end result is achieved.

The physical changes that are involved in puberty lead to a very important result — adult men and women with fully mature bodies that are capable of procreation. You are growing toward this goal, but this growth takes place over a number of years.

Some people find it helpful to think of puberty as something that happens in stages:

AGE	CHILDHOOD	PUBERTY BEGINS	ADOLESCENCE

Each figure represents ten percent of all the people in that age group

STAGE 1	The pituitary begins to secrete hormones. Changes begin to happen within your body, but you don't even notice them. This is because there are no outward signs of development.
STAGE 2	Now the body shape of boys and girls begins to change. Boys may notice that their testicles and scrotum have begun to grow, and girls will notice that their breasts have begun to develop. During this stage girls' height and weight increase quite rapidly, and the shape of the body changes as fat is deposited on the hips. Both sexes may have a small amount of pubic hair.
STAGE 3	By this stage of puberty, boys and girls are beginning to look more like young adults. The male reproductive organs continue to grow and more pubic hair develops. The boy's shoulders become broader, his muscles develop, he gains height quickly, and his voice begins to deepen. The girl's breasts continue to develop, pubic hair increases, and her hips widen. Toward the end of this stage girls may experience the signs of cycling and fertility for the first time — menstruation and the presence of cervical mucus.
STAGE 4	It is during this stage that most boys experience their first nocturnal emission, which is a sign of their developing fertility. The voice continues to deepen and underarm hair begins to grow. During this stage most boys develop hair on their upper lip, and possibly on their chins. If girls have not already menstruated, they usually begin during this stage and ovulation may occur during some cycles. Underarm hair begins to grow, and breast and hip development continue.
STAGE 5	During the last stage of puberty, the physical changes are completed. By the end of this stage both sexes have fully developed reproductive systems, and their bodies have the appearance of adult males and females. Young men usually begin shaving during this stage. They may grow a little bit taller, but their growth spurt is over. Young women have reached their full height and are menstruating and ovulating quite regularly.

Because there are such differences in the rate of development during puberty, young adolescents often worry about whether they are normal. Early development seems to be especially difficult for girls, and late development especially difficult for boys. It's not easy to be different, but it is perfectly normal to develop quickly or slowly, early or late. Most boys and girls, however, are more likely to be somewhere in the middle.

All young people have some feelings of confusion, worry, embarrassment, and shyness about their bodies. It takes time and patience to become comfortable with the physical changes of puberty. Understanding these changes can make it a little easier, but the task of becoming physically mature young men and women who are comfortable with their new bodies is always a challenging one.

We have been describing the human body and its physical development during puberty. But it is important to remember that whenever we talk about the body, we are talking about persons. The body is not a thing that we carry around as if it were not really part of us. The person is a body-spirit. We experience the world through our bodies. We respond to other people through our bodies. We express our thoughts and feelings through our bodies. Whatever we know and experience is known and experienced through the body.

Beyond this human experience, our faith expands our understanding of the body. God became one of us and lived as a person with a human body. Jesus experienced the physical changes of puberty. He lived in relationship with others, had human feelings, and experienced pleasure and pain through his body. Because of his life, death, and resurrection, we know that the whole person, the body-spirit, is intended for eternal life.

As we discover more about the body, we learn to appreciate its complex and beautiful design. We come to value and protect our fertility. We are content to accept our bodies, with all their beauty and with their imperfections. We respect and honour our bodies as a gift from God, in whose image we are made.

Relating as Sexual People

As you go through puberty, you may sometimes wonder if you will ever feel normal again. At times it will seem as if everything in your life is changing. Your body is developing, your moods can be unstable, your relationships with parents and friends are changing, and there are new concerns about sexual identity. You may also have a new awareness of the opposite sex, and many new questions.

It takes time and patience to become comfortable with the "new" you. But it is good to remember that you also remain the same person that you always were, even though the many changes in your life may make that hard for you to believe. The experiences you have had as a boy or a girl, your friendships, your relationships with your family members, the interests you have developed, and your personality traits are always part of you. As you grow and develop during adolescence, you will be building on the foundation of the person that you already are.

Sexual Attraction

Sexual attraction is a wonderful part of the gift of sexuality, but it is also confusing when it is first experienced. There is a strong physical-spiritual attraction between males and females. This attraction draws men and women together, and leads them to develop a personal relationship. It encourages them to learn to know each other, to share their experiences, and to discover how they complement each other.

Sometime during adolescence, you will discover that you have become more aware of members of the opposite sex. You notice their appearance and the way they act, and you wonder whether they notice you. Then, when they do pay attention to you, you may feel awkward or shy. You're not sure how to behave. Sometimes you embarrass yourself by the way you act. You get tongue-tied, talk too much, get silly, or show off.

You may like one particular person and spend a lot of time thinking about that person. You imagine what it would be like to get to know him or her. You feel anxious, excited, happy, and restless all at the same time. The other person may not even be aware of you, but that doesn't change your feelings. You begin to wonder — is this what falling in love is like? The answer is yes, but it's the very first stage of falling in love, and there are many others. Some people describe these feelings as infatuation. When you're infatuated with someone, you have very intense feelings about the person, but these feelings don't occur in response to knowing the person. In fact, if you got to know the person you might discover that you have very little in common. First infatuations usually don't last too long, and several months later you might find yourself infatuated with someone else.

Sometimes young people also have very strong feelings about someone of the same sex. It is often someone they admire very much and want to be like. This is a normal part of development, especially in early adolescence. If this has happened to you, you might be wondering if it means that you are a homosexual. At your stage in life, having strong feelings for someone of the same sex does not indicate homosexuality. You are going through a period when you have intense feelings about many things. Your likes and dislikes are very strong, and you are just beginning to discover how overpowering your feelings about other people can be. This experience is part of maturing, and learning to be a man or woman.

Until now your closest friendships have been with members of your own sex. These relationships will continue to deepen and become even more important to you. As sexual attraction draws you toward the opposite sex, you will need to remember that a relationship cannot be built on sexual attraction alone. It's a wonderful feeling to be intensely attracted to another person. It may happen many times during your teenage years. The feelings are meant to be enjoyed, but it's important to keep them in perspective. Friendship between males and females requires time and effort, trust, shared interests, a willingness to reveal oneself, and an appreciation of each other's qualities.

Dear Anna,

Happy twentieth anniversary! I wonder if you are as amazed to read that number as I am to write it. Those twenty years have seemed like twenty days. Here I am, a father of three and middle-aged already. I know that happens to others, but I didn't think it would happen to me. Wasn't I supposed to stay twenty-seven forever? I may not look like him, but I still often feel like the uncertain and self-doubting young man who met you so long ago. Do you remember how serious I was? I didn't know who I really was or what I wanted to do with my life. But I did know that I wanted to know you better. And I found that as I got to know you, and then to love you, and could feel your love for me, I discovered who I was and what I could do. Now, more than twenty years later, I want to tell you again that I love you, that my love for you is so deeply a part of me that it flows through me like a heartbeat, that my knowing that you love me makes my life joyful.

We've had many good times together and a few bad ones, and our share of successes and failures. But I wouldn't trade a minute of the last twenty years. It's all been a journey I wouldn't have missed for the world. I don't know what the next twenty years will bring, but I keep thinking, with pleasure and excitement, of the poem by Browning that contains the lines:

"Grow old along with me,
The best is yet to be. . . "
Will you join me?

                    Your loving husband,
                    Len

Respect for Self and Others

As you mature, you will have some difficult choices to make. Making choices is part of the responsibility of being human. We are created free, and can use our freedom to choose wisely or unwisely. Some of your choices will involve sexuality and your relationships with other people. When you come to make decisions about the way you are going to use the gift of your sexuality, you will need to remember that it is persons who are sexual, not just their bodies. We cannot claim to have respect for persons, but, through our actions and words, show disrespect for their bodies.

Respect for the gift of sexuality is called *chastity*. Chastity is the virtue that helps us to live as sexual persons in the way that God intends. Everyone is called to be chaste, but each according to her or his state in life. For married people, sexual intercourse is a sign of their total commitment, and the virtue of chastity helps husbands and wives to be loving and faithful to each other. For single people, respect for the gift of sexuality excludes an intimate sexual relationship.

It is not always easy to be chaste. Because we are human, we have many powerful feelings and urges. Some of these are sexual — our desire for intimacy, for completion, for human contact, and for sexual pleasure. But we have to direct and control these feelings. Prayer and regular reception of the sacrament of Reconciliation can be a powerful help as we strive to develop the Christian virtue of chastity. We can always ask for God's help to express our feelings in a way that respects the gift of sexuality in ourselves and in others.

Some Serious Abuses of Sexuality

When we ignore God's plan for us as human persons and use our gifts in selfish and uncaring ways, we are abusing those gifts. Sexuality is so powerful and so central to who we are, that its abuse can result in great harm to ourselves and others.

Rape

Sexual assault is a terrible crime of violence. When a male or female is forced or intimidated into sexual intimacy of any kind by another person, a serious abuse of sexuality has occurred. Actions that are intended to express love and commitment instead express aggression and domination. The victim of a sexual assault has been treated as if he or she were an object, rather than a human person.

Sexual intercourse that is forced on a female against her will is known as *rape*. Rape is a serious abuse of sexuality and a crime of violence. Sexual intercourse is meant to be a sign of a deeply committed and freely given love between a husband and wife, not a sign of power and force. Females who have been raped suffer a terrifying, humiliating, and destructive experience, and are often in need of counselling to help them recover.

Sexual Abuse of Children

One of the most serious abuses of sexuality occurs when an adult involves a child or young teen-ager in intimate physical sexual activity. In many cases, sadly, the adult is someone whom the child or teen-ager knows well and should be able to trust. It is for this reason that the sexual abuse of children is so destructive. It destroys trust. It violates a child's right to grow up in a safe, loving environment.

When sexual activity occurs between members of the same family, it is called *incest*. The most frequent type of incest occurs between an older male relative (father, step-father, uncle, older brother) and a young girl. Incest not only harms the child or young teen-ager who is the victim, but it also harms the whole family.

Because children lack the maturity to give full consent to sexual activity with an adult, they are not to blame for the situation, even though they may feel guilty. Those who have been sexually abused by adults have had a terrible wrong done to them. They need to tell someone they trust about what has happened. If the first person they confide in does not believe them or cannot help them, then they must find another person. There is help available to victims of sexual abuse, but they have to take the first step by telling someone about the abuse.

As sexual development takes place during puberty, new sensations and urges are experienced in the body. Many adolescents discover that touching their genitals gives them a new kind of pleasure, one which they have not experienced before. Deliberately touching yourself in order to give yourself sexual pleasure is called masturbation. It is a difficult subject for people to talk about because it is so private. Also, sometimes people find it embarrassing or shameful.

It is natural to be curious about your developing body and its new sensations. It is also necessary to develop habits of self-control. As you mature you will grow in your understanding that sexuality is relational, not solitary. Masturbation leads people into self-centredness, rather than outward toward other people.

Some young people can find it very difficult to avoid masturbating, but it is important to struggle with this issue, and to ask for God's help. Sexual pleasure is a wonderful gift that each person must learn to understand and respect. It is one of the many gifts that a man and a woman experience and offer each other within the committed relationship of marriage.

Sexuality and Decision-making

Adolescence is meant to be a time for exploring different friendships, discovering more about yourself, and making plans for your future. It is a special time between childhood and adulthood when you become comfortable with your new body, secure in your sexual identity, and learn to make decisions that reflect your values and your stage of development.

Your life is stretching out in front of you, like a long road. At each side of the road there are some turns that you might take in the next several years. Some of these turns are detours. Before long they lead you back to the main road. A detour in a young person's life might be a friendship that didn't work out, a difficult experience with a teacher, or a stressful situation at home.

But there are other turns off this main road that lead to dead ends. Almost all young adolescents understand that it is not the right time in their lives for an intimate sexual relationship. They know that it will be many years before they are ready for the total friendship and committed relationship of marriage. Yet some people become sexually active when they are very young, and many more do so a few years later.

Intimate sexual activity prevents young people from developing deep relationships, and exposes them to the serious dangers of sexually transmitted diseases, as well as endangering their fertility. Also, there is always the possibility of pregnancy, a responsibility that young people are not ready to accept. A sexual relationship may seem like a short-cut to intimacy, but it is really a dead end. It is not part of God's plan that young people should harm themselves in this way.

It is difficult for people to make a decision about sexual activity in a situation where they feel pressured, or are sexually aroused. The body responds on its own, and after a certain amount of time, kissing and touching lead to intercourse. The decision not to be sexually active has to be made earlier so that young people will avoid such situations.

As well, young adolescents need to develop the confidence to say no. This decision does not have to be explained or defended. No one has the right to pressure another person into sexual activity, and if someone tries to, the response should be clear and final.

Some young people do travel down a side road, reach a dead end, and have to turn around and come back to the main road. It can be very hard, but it is never impossible. We are always offered another chance to make a good decision. God is always ready to forgive us and give us a new start.

99

During this time of life, self-acceptance, self-esteem, and self-respect are very important qualities for you to develop and nurture. If you accept yourself as the unique male or female that you are, you are less likely to look for acceptance through sexual activity. If you believe in yourself and know your own value, you will have the confidence to withstand sexual pressures and to say no. If you respect yourself as a male or female, you will be able to offer others the respect they deserve.

The adults who care about you want to help you during the next years of your life. There will be times when you will consider their help an interference. They cannot force you to take their advice, but they can share with you their experiences of growing up. They want you to have a happy and a safe journey to adulthood.

Even with strong personal qualities and the support of adults, you will still have some difficult times along the way. That is the way it is for everyone. The responsibility to understand the place of sexuality in your relationships is a very challenging one. You need other people in your life to guide you, comfort you when things go badly, and give you the courage to keep on trying. You need to follow God's plan for human sexuality so that you will not harm yourself or others. You are created sexual for a reason — to be a loving, life-giving person, a reflection of the One who made you.

call Chris!

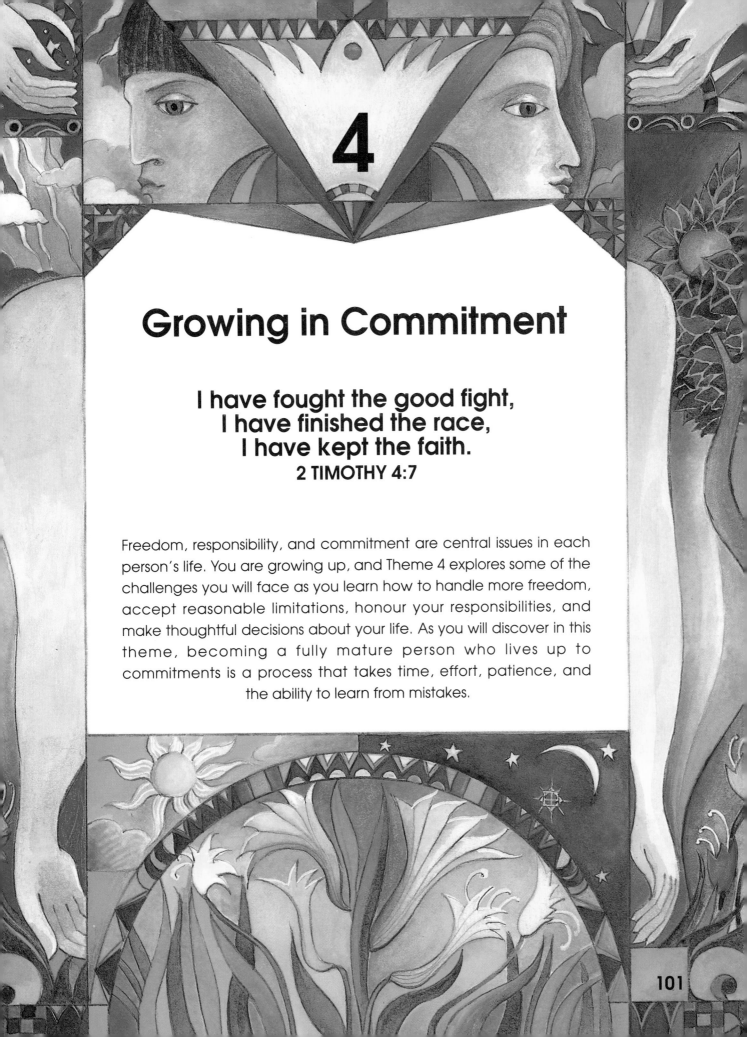

4

Growing in Commitment

**I have fought the good fight,
I have finished the race,
I have kept the faith.**
2 TIMOTHY 4:7

Freedom, responsibility, and commitment are central issues in each person's life. You are growing up, and Theme 4 explores some of the challenges you will face as you learn how to handle more freedom, accept reasonable limitations, honour your responsibilities, and make thoughtful decisions about your life. As you will discover in this theme, becoming a fully mature person who lives up to commitments is a process that takes time, effort, patience, and the ability to learn from mistakes.

Growing Up

How do you feel about growing up?

• "I can't wait. No one to tell me what to do!" (Sean, Grade 5)

• "I don't think I like it. My friends are no fun anymore. They put on make-up after school, and then stand on the street corner and smoke. This has been the worst year of my life." (Marlene, Grade 8)

• "Sometimes I think I would like things to stay just the way they are. I've got great friends, I enjoy school, and I get along pretty well with my parents." (Tony, Grade 11)

From a distance, being grown up looks very easy and appealing. Young children often assume that adults have all the answers, and can do whatever they want. All that freedom, and no responsibilities.

Of course, as you know, it's not that simple. Despite their life experience adults still have unanswered questions, and their freedom to act and make decisions is balanced with many responsibilities.

Growing up is a process. There is no magic moment when a person says, "Ah, now I have finished growing up." Many people in their thirties, forties, and older are surprised by the way they continue to mature, learn, develop new interests, and discover aspects of themselves they did not recognize earlier.

• "I'm not sure. I wish I knew what I'm going to do with my life. I'd like some time to travel and see the world. I want to figure out who I am." (Jessica, Second year university student)

102

There is a special time of growth, however, during which people mature by leaps and bounds. At the beginning of this period they are children; some eight to ten years later, they are adults. There are remarkable changes during the life-stage of adolescence, and all aspects of development are affected — physical, intellectual, social, emotional and spiritual.

From childhood to adulthood is a big step.

Adolescence is the life stage during which people learn how to be adults. It is a time for developing the inner strength that will allow you to be your own person — a person of honesty, integrity, and faithfulness. In order for this to happen you will need:
• a variety of experiences, and relationships with many different people
• guidance from others, and the opportunity to make decisions for yourself
• the courage to take responsibility for yourself, and the ability to learn from mistakes
• a deep commitment to your faith, and strong Christian values.

You are at the beginning of this process. As you look ahead, your thoughts may be mostly positive, mostly negative, or a mixture. The word that best describes the way many people your age feel about growing up is *ambivalence*.

Ambivalence means having mixed emotions or feelings, which pull you in opposite directions.

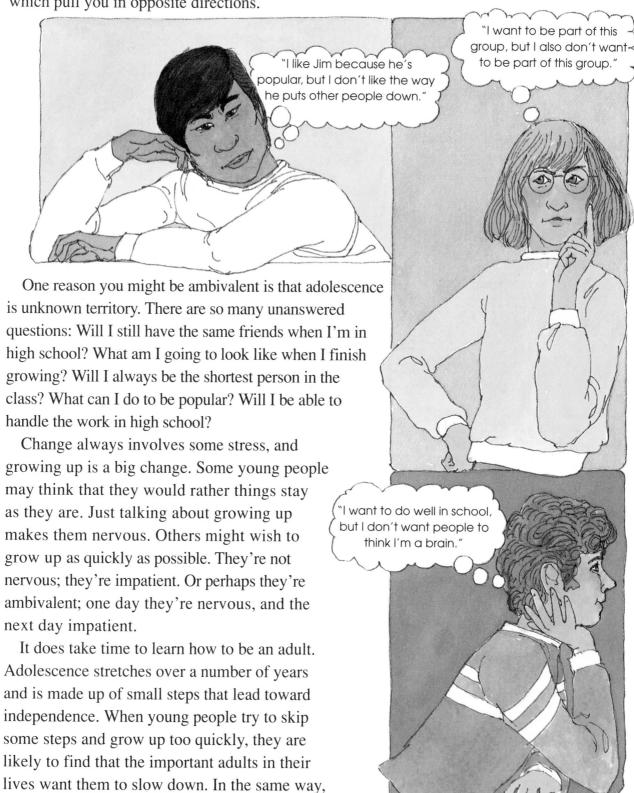

One reason you might be ambivalent is that adolescence is unknown territory. There are so many unanswered questions: Will I still have the same friends when I'm in high school? What am I going to look like when I finish growing? Will I always be the shortest person in the class? What can I do to be popular? Will I be able to handle the work in high school?

Change always involves some stress, and growing up is a big change. Some young people may think that they would rather things stay as they are. Just talking about growing up makes them nervous. Others might wish to grow up as quickly as possible. They're not nervous; they're impatient. Or perhaps they're ambivalent; one day they're nervous, and the next day impatient.

It does take time to learn how to be an adult. Adolescence stretches over a number of years and is made up of small steps that lead toward independence. When young people try to skip some steps and grow up too quickly, they are likely to find that the important adults in their lives want them to slow down. In the same way, if an adolescent is hesitant about moving along the road to maturity, parents or teachers may give a small nudge.

New Responsibilities, New Freedom

When you were an infant, it could be said that you had no freedom and no responsibilities. You were completely dependent on your parents. One way of thinking about your life since those early days is that it has been a process of gaining both responsibilities and freedom. For example, when you first learned to dress yourself, you acquired a freedom that you didn't have before. You didn't have to depend on an adult in order to get dressed. But you also gained a responsibility. If you complained that you wanted help getting dressed, your mother or father probably reminded you that you that could do it yourself.

As people mature they become more and more independent and are capable of assuming greater responsibilities. Additional tasks at home, babysitting, small part-time jobs in the neighbourhood, refereeing a game for younger students, volunteer work in the community — these activities are all opportunities to become more dependable and more self-directed.

But responsibilities do have to be in line with an individual's ability and maturity. Too little or too much responsibility can lead to problems.

• Brian is thirteen. His mother makes his bed for him, and looks underneath for his dirty laundry. She checks his knapsack before she goes to bed and puts in the books he needs for school the next day. She wakes him up in the morning and spends the next hour telling him to hurry up or he'll be late. His father usually drives Brian to school in order to get him there on time. What do you think is going to happen to Brian in the future?

• Lisa is thirteen. She babysits for a neighbour almost every Friday night. The children she cares for are quite young and are usually in bed by the time she arrives to babysit. The neighbour is going away for the week-end and would like Lisa to look after the children from Friday evening until Sunday afternoon. Lisa is anxious to do this. Should she?

Freedom and responsibility go together. Freedom includes the power to make your own choices and decisions. It also involves accepting responsibility for these decisions.

At this point in your life, there are two important limitations on your freedom:

• The first limitation comes from outside of you — the restrictions that adults, and especially parents, place on you.

• The second limitation comes from inside you. It takes maturity and experience to take on big responsibilities and to make important decisions independently. When parents limit young people's freedom it is a way of protecting them as they grow up. Sometimes people your age argue that they will never learn to be responsible and to make good decisions unless they have the opportunity to try. It's a good argument. Young adolescents do need the chance to make some decisions, to take on new responsibilities, and to make some mistakes. What's important to parents is that these mistakes be small detours, not dead ends that are going to be harmful.

Making Decisions

As you go through adolescence, your goal is to be in charge of yourself and to take responsibility for your decisions, not just in day-to-day matters, but in important issues that will have an impact on your future life. You will still want to seek advice from family members and other people whose opinion you value. They may suggest options or point out consequences that you haven't considered.

But no matter what approach people take to decision making, there are some do's and don't's that are important for everyone to remember:

Tina's dad sent her some money for her birthday. Her plan was to save for a pair of boots that her mother had said were too expensive. Her mom agreed that if Tina could save another ten dollars, she would share the cost of the boots. On Saturday Tina went shopping and had the birthday money in her wallet. She saw two tapes that she wanted and decided to buy them. It wasn't until she got home that she thought about the boots.

DON'T — be an impulsive decision-maker.

Mark has a social studies project due in several days. There was a list of topics to choose from, and he is still trying to make up his mind which one to do. He has done some research on three different topics. Topic 1 appears interesting, but there are no books left in the school library on this topic and only one in the public library. Topic 2 is quite difficult, and Topic 3 seems easy, but boring. Mark is beginning to worry that he won't finish his project on time.

DO — set a time limit for making a decision.

Mai wanted to earn some extra money and decided to get a morning paper route.

She has to start very early and she agreed that she would set an alarm and get up independently. Her grandmother and her parents reminded her that she doesn't like to get up in the morning, and 6:00 a.m. is very early. Mai has had the paper route for two weeks, and so far she has slept through her alarm twice. On both occasions she had stayed up too late the night before. There have been some complaints from customers about late papers. She is also finding it difficult to concentrate at school since she rarely finds time for breakfast.

DO — expect to make mistakes.

Tina has earned some money from babysitting and from looking after a neighbour's cat. She has given the money to her mother to keep. "I don't want to be tempted to spend it on tapes or junk food," she said. "I want to save for those boots."

Mark has decided that the next time he has a choice of topics, he will make a decision at least one week before the project has to be ready. He has put a calendar in his room to keep track of the dates for assignments.

Mai has quit her morning paper route, and applied for an afternoon one. She can't get as long a route, so she will earn less, but the alarm no longer rings at 6:00 a.m.

DO — learn from your mistakes

110

Not all decisions are complicated or require a great deal of thought. But for decisions that have a lot of options or are quite important, there is a process you can follow. For example, Chris has a difficult decision to make. He is in Grade 8 and his family has to move by the end of February. They will be living about a hundred kilometres from their present home. Chris would like to stay in the same school and graduate with his class. This would be possible if he lives at his grandmother's house during the week and goes home only on week-ends. His parents have discussed the situation and are agreed that this is a decision he can make for himself. They are ready to offer him advice, as are his friends. He lies awake at night thinking about what he should do. One day he decides to live at his grandmother's, the next day he changes his mind. He wants to make a good decision, but he's feeling quite confused.

Making a Decision

Step 1: Find a time when you're not busy and can concentrate on the situation that requires a decision.

Step 2: Describe the situation that needs a decision.

My parents are moving and I don't want to change schools in the middle of the school year.

Step 3: What are your options?

1. Move with my parents.
2. Live with my grandmother and go home on week-ends.
3. Live at home and commute each day to school by bus or train.

Step 4: Evaluate your options. What are the pros and cons? What are the possible consequences? Are these consequences acceptable to you?

OPTION 1:   MOVE WITH MY PARENTS.

Pros

I'll be with my family.

Cons

I'd miss my friends.
I won't graduate with my friends.
I'd have to get used to a new school, and I'd only be there a few months.

Possible Consequences

I might be really lonely because I wouldn't have much of a chance to make new friends.

OPTION 2:   LIVE WITH MY GRANDMOTHER, GO HOME ON WEEK-ENDS.

Pros

I'd be with my friends.
I'd graduate with my class.

Cons

I'd miss my family.
My grandmother is much stricter than my parents.

Possible Consequences

I might be really unhappy without my family. My family will miss me. My grandmother and I might not get along. I will have less freedom at my grandmother's.

112

OPTION 3: LIVE AT HOME AND COMMUTE TO SCHOOL.

Pros

I could live at home and go to my old school.

Cons

Very expensive.
I would spend a lot of time travelling.
I wouldn't have much time to see my friends because I have to get the bus to go home.
I couldn't do my after-school activities.

Possible Consequences

I might get fed up with all that travelling.

Step 5: Consider the options and choose the one that seems to be best.

My decision is to live with my grandmother.

Step 6: Some time later, review your decision. Was it a good decision? Are you happy with it? If not, can you change it?

****

Chris found this process for making his decision much better than lying in bed worrying. Many people find that they can't solve problems when they're tired or preoccupied. That is why Step 1 is so important.

When Chris came to Step 3 and listed his options, he included a third option that his older brother suggested. It's a good idea to ask your family members or other people whose opinions you value if they can think of any options you may have overlooked. But when he talked to his parents about the idea of living at home and commuting to school, he discovered that it wasn't really an option. His parents said that it was simply too expensive.

A month has gone by since Chris' family moved. He does miss his family, and he and his grandmother have had some disagreements about when he should go to bed, and what clothes he wears to school. But when they are not disagreeing, they are getting to know each other better. He is very happy to see his parents on the week-ends, and he enjoys all the attention he gets.

Making thoughtful decisions is a skill that people can learn. Math problems can't be solved without learning the correct procedure. If you leave out one of the steps, you end up with the wrong answer. It's the same with decisions. When people ignore consequences, they get unpleasant surprises. If they forget to consider all their options, they may miss the one that's just right for them. But the most important reason for developing the ability to make thoughtful decisions is that it helps you to become a responsible person.

"Why are adults always nagging about responsibility?"

Responsibility and Commitment

Adults consider it important for young people to be growing in the direction of responsibility and commitment because these are essential qualities of a fully mature person. At times they may lecture (or nag) and expect too much, but the alternative — to have no expectations or give no guidance — would be irresponsible on their part. Everyone matures physically without any guidance from anyone. Physical maturation simply happens. The pituitary gland releases its hormones and the body begins to change. Once these changes are completed, the result is a fully mature adult male or female body.

"My dad's always talking about being more dependable and reliable."

"I want to have fun and enjoy life."

"My teacher's favourite word is responsibility."

But unlike physical maturation, becoming a fully mature *person* is not automatic. You can't just sit around waiting to become an adult. It is an accomplishment; you have to do something to make it happen. It is also an accomplishment that cannot be achieved alone. It requires personal effort and determination, the experience of relating to other people, guidance from those who are fully mature, and the grace of God.

Responsible and Committed People

A sense of responsibility doesn't develop in isolation. When other people respect and encourage us, we come to understand our responsibility to respect and believe in ourselves. We develop the self-confidence to reach out to other people and to accept the responsibilities that are part of all relationships.

There are several ways of examining responsibilities. You could make a list and include each activity in which you participate from the time you get up until you go to bed. If you filled in this list over several weeks, you would have a record of many of your responsibilities.

Another way would be to look at different areas of your life — home, school, parish, friends, special activities, and community — and reflect on the responsibilities you have in each of these areas. But perhaps the best place to begin is with yourself and the responsibilities you have toward that person. Here are some items you might include:

- to be good to myself because I am a valuable person whom God loves
- to recognize and develop my talents, and to share them with others
- to recognize my faults, and to try to overcome them
- to grow in self-understanding, self-honesty, and self-respect
- to deepen my relationship with God through prayer
- to deepen my relationships with those people who are an important part of my life.

Myself
Home
School
Friends
Parish
Special Activities
Community

As you think about different responsibilities in your life, you may notice that many of them involve relationships. This is because relationships are so central to who we are — sons, daughters, husbands, wives, mothers, fathers, students, teachers, friends, and Christians.

When you discussed relationships earlier you learned that they may be superficial, intimate, or somewhere in between. Your responsibilities toward other people depend on the depth of your relationship and on its nature.

Some relationships are very intimate and involve many responsibilities. People often speak of their deepest relationships as commitments. There are some people in your life who are so important to you, and you are so important to them that you cannot imagine your life without them, and they cannot imagine their lives without you. This doesn't mean that these relationships always go smoothly or are without conflict. *Being* committed and *feeling* committed are not the same thing.

Being committed means that even though you feel angry, hurt, disappointed, and frustrated with one of your parents, a sister or brother, or a close friend, you don't give up on that person. You go on loving the person even though she or he is not very loveable at that moment, and you continue to recognize your responsibilities toward that person.

What are Angie's responsibilities toward the man behind the counter? Should she confide in him, or offer her help with the work of running the store? Does she have a responsibility to pay for the milk, and to wait in line until it's her turn? What are the clerk's responsibilities toward Angie?

Take out the garbage.

Clean my room once
a week.

Do my homework.

Come home in time
for dinner.

Help with the dishes.

Are these the only responsibilities
that are involved in an intimate
relationship?

Most students your age and many adults would produce lists of
family responsibilities like Bill's. Because there are so many
tasks that have to be accomplished each day, we tend to see our
family responsibilities as a series of chores — cooking,
cleaning, washing dishes, shopping, doing laundry, disposing
of garbage, and making beds. Family members do have a
responsibility to participate in these tasks, to share the work,
and to do these chores as cheerfully and willingly as they can.

But commitment to family is much deeper than daily or
weekly chores. It includes responsibilities like:
• being open with each other
• listening to each other
• enjoying each other
• participating in activities together
• depending on each other
• resolving conflicts
• making a consistent effort to understand the point of view
  of each family member.
This last responsibility — trying to understand each other's
point of view — is especially important for parents and
young adolescents.

Parents have a responsibility to recognize young people's need to make some decisions, to try to understand their ambivalence about growing up, and to negotiate with them over the issue of independence. At the same time, young people have a responsibility to try to understand their parents' perspective. You may not realize it, but many parents also feel ambivalent as their children reach adolescence:

"I want her to be more independent, but I worry about big problems like drugs, alcohol, and sex."

"You can't keep them young forever, but there are times when I wish you could."

"I feel sad sometimes when I see how grown-up he is."

When both parents and children are committed to trying to understand each other, their relationship is strengthened. They listen to each other's point of view, and while they don't always agree, they continue to listen to each other. They recognize that they have a responsibility to handle their changing relationship with patience, fairness, respect, loyalty, and a sense of humour.

Commitment to Friends

When your friendships are going well, you're not likely to think of them as responsibilities. You enjoy being with your friends, have common interests, go places together, and confide in each other. But these normal friendship activities are also responsibilities. You have to be willing to:

Spend time together.

Learn more about each other's interests.

Be open with each other.

Participate in activities together.

Try to understand each other's perspective.

The commitment of friendship also involves loyalty. When friends have a serious disagreement, they have a responsibility to discuss what led to the disagreement and to search for a solution. Loyalty toward friends also involves faithfulness. Friends have a responsibility to keep their word, not to gossip about each other, and to accept each other's faults and occasional bad moods.

But loyalty doesn't mean ownership, exclusiveness, or giving up values. Because relationships with friends often change and grow more intense during adolescence, loyalty can be misunderstood and become a problem:

• One person tries to control the relationship.

• A good friend starts to spend time with another person.

"Mike and Jim are together a lot, so I guess Mike doesn't want to be friends with me anymore."

• Loyalty to friends leads to doing something that is wrong.

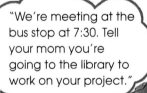

"We're meeting at the bus stop at 7:30. Tell your mom you're going to the library to work on your project."

Each of these situations involves a misunderstanding of commitment in friendship.

The first two situations are very similar. What is being overlooked is that friendship is a chosen relationship, and therefore has to be free. You can't make someone be your friend, or prevent a person from being friends with someone else. Even an intimate friendship doesn't exclude others.

The third situation involves a different kind of misunderstanding. Loyalty toward friends is important, but it has to be balanced with other responsibilities. Peer pressure can be hard to withstand without a strong commitment to think and act as individuals and to behave in a way that reflects our values. When loyalty to friends becomes more important than this commitment to ourselves, there is a lack of balance in our lives that needs attention.

121

Balancing Responsibilities

We all have difficulties at one time or another handling our responsibilities. Sometimes it's because we have too many, but most often it's because we don't spend enough time thinking about the need for balance in our lives.

How would you describe a well-balanced person? Someone who spends some time on work, some on play, some with friends, and some with family members? Dividing up time among various responsibilities is certainly part of being a well-balanced person. When one part of people's lives consumes almost all of their time, then they are probably overlooking some of their responsibilities. For example, people who spend most of the week-end watching television are probably neglecting their commitment to family members and friends.

Balancing responsibilities is really a way of balancing yourself. Here are some points to consider:
- Are you developing all aspects of your life — physical, intellectual, emotional, social, and spiritual?
- Do you spend some time alone, some with family members, and some with friends?
- Do you give yourself fully to whatever you are doing — school work, talking to a friend, helping out at home, after-school activities, teams, clubs, hobbies, etc?

It's not always easy to become a well-balanced person. Sometimes people ignore certain responsibilities because they dislike them or find them too challenging. Bill, for example, finds most school work boring and often avoids doing his homework or participating in class discussion.

A Well-Balanced Saturday

Morning

1. Get up by 9.00 (NO LATER)

2. Go to the library and see if they still need volunteers to help with the pre-school story hour. Also look for books for my history project.

Afternoon

3. Do math homework

4. Help Mom clean the basement.

5. Meet Tina at 5.00 and go to Tracey's house for dinner.

Evening

6. Stay at Tracey's till Mom picks me up. Try not to be shy with Tracey's parents. Be nice to Tina.

7. Start reading for my history project if I can keep awake

Angie is very shy and dislikes social situations that involve groups of people. If she isn't with Tracey, she tends to spend her free time watching television or reading. She rarely gets exercise, and she avoids her responsibility to develop the social aspect of her life. How can she become a more well-balanced person?

Becoming a responsible and commited person is a long process. It takes time to learn how to make good decisions, to accept responsibility, and to keep your life in balance. Mistakes are inevitable; no one grows up without making mistakes. One of your responsibilities is to be patient with yourself. You have never been a young adolescent before. It's important to be heading in the right direction. You are working at being a person who is growing in commitment — to God, to yourself, and to other people.

"Between the great things we cannot do, and the little things we will not do, the danger is that we will do nothing." (H. G. Weaver)

"Duty does not have to be dull. Love can make it beautiful and fill it with life." (Thomas Merton)

"Every day is a messenger of God." (Russian proverb)

"Faithfulness in little things is a big thing." (St. John Chrysostom)

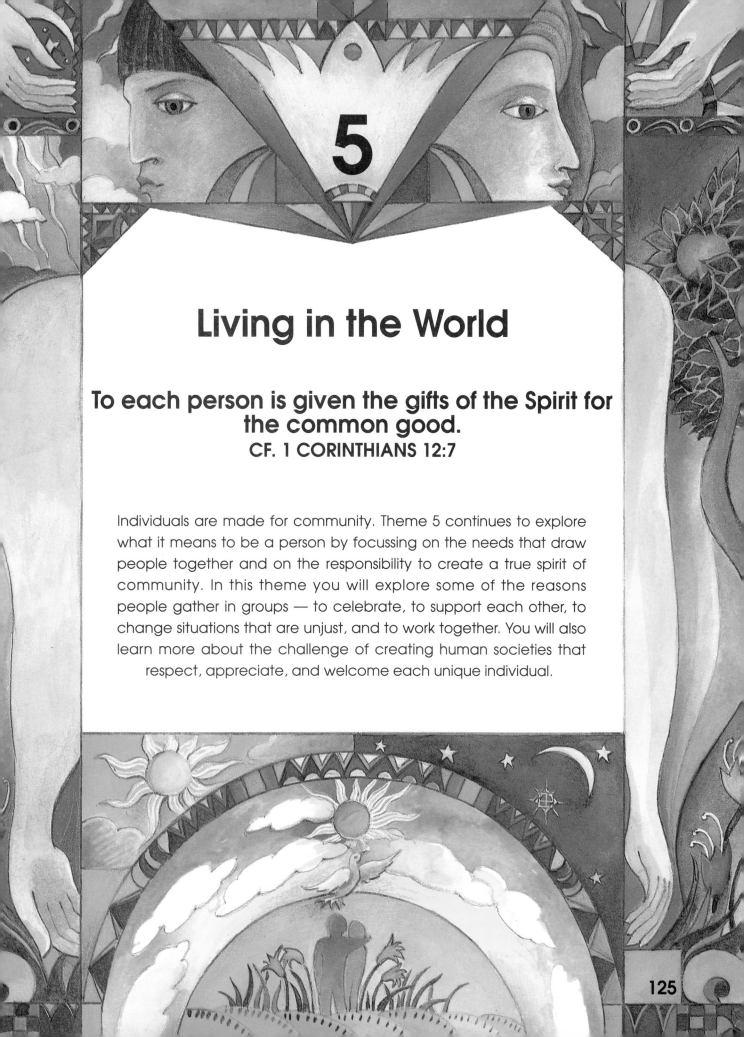

Living in the World

To each person is given the gifts of the Spirit for the common good.
CF. 1 CORINTHIANS 12:7

Individuals are made for community. Theme 5 continues to explore what it means to be a person by focussing on the needs that draw people together and on the responsibility to create a true spirit of community. In this theme you will explore some of the reasons people gather in groups — to celebrate, to support each other, to change situations that are unjust, and to work together. You will also learn more about the challenge of creating human societies that respect, appreciate, and welcome each unique individual.

We Gather Together

We are social beings and we are drawn together by our common experiences, needs, and responsibilities. It is part of our human nature to live in relationship with others, and to gather together in groups.

"I am a Canadian."

There are many different kinds of groups, some with thousands of members, some with only five or six members. There are groups that have been around for hundreds of years, and others that have just been formed.

Some groups are so important to us that they are part of our identity — our membership in a family, in a country, in a faith community. In many cases, our membership in these groups is not something that we chose, but something that was given to us at birth.

Another kind of group lasts just for a short period of time. For example, Mr. Dryden asked for volunteers to plan a class picnic. Five students were interested and they met twice as a group. When they had decided on a location and a menu, and planned the activities, their work was done and there was no need for the group to meet again.

"I am a Catholic."

"I am an Ojibway."

"I am Korean."

"I am a McPherson."

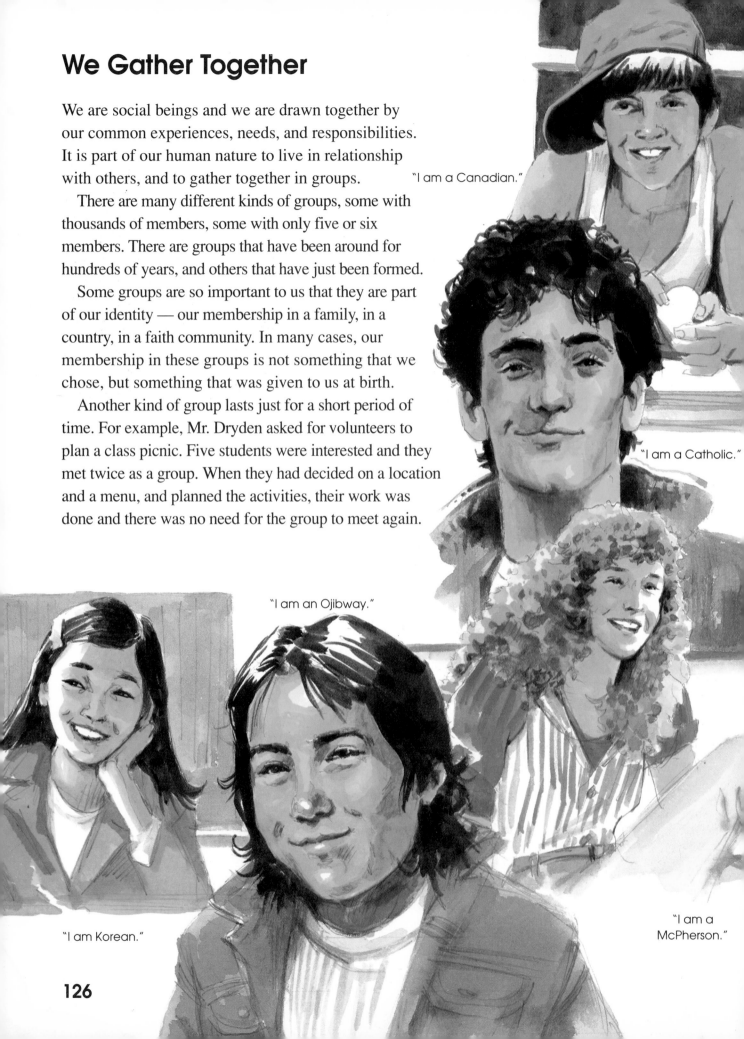

126

There are other groups that last for a long time, but their membership changes regularly. If you were a Cub Scout or a Brownie when you were younger, you probably belonged for two or three years. But the Scouts or Brownies didn't stop when you left. Or perhaps you are a member of a team or club that is very important to you right now. Your interests could change, however, and next year you might decide to try a new activity. But the club or team will continue even though you're no longer a member.

Every group has a purpose, a reason that its members come together. It could be to enjoy a special interest or develop a talent that is not shared by large numbers of people. Or perhaps the reason for membership is based on a unique personal characteristic.

A sky-diving club is an example of a group based on a special interest.

But as well as special interests, talents, and personal characteristics, there are also human needs, experiences, and responsibilities that we all share, and which draw us together as members of the human family. We are created to find fulfillment with each other. We need to share ourselves, to enjoy each other's company, to learn from each other's experiences, and to work together to create a society that is respectful, generous, peaceful, and just. This is true whether we are talking about the family, the parish community, the neighbourhood, the classroom, the school, the country, or any other group in which people gather together.

We Celebrate Together

Some things are so important and have so much meaning for us that we celebrate them. In small or large groups, we gather together to show our pride in membership and to express our shared values and beliefs.

It's difficult to celebrate alone. When something is important to us, or when we are bursting with pride and joy, we want to be with others to share our feelings.

We usually think of celebrations as joyful occasions, and most often they are. But there are some celebrations that are touched, or even filled, with sadness. The most obvious example is the death of a family member or close friend. People gather together not only to mourn and to pray, but also to celebrate the life of the person who has died. They want to join with others who knew and loved the person, share their memories, and laugh and cry together. They are celebrating an earthly life that has come to an end, and the beginning of eternal life with God.

We first learn to celebrate in the small community of the family. Births, deaths, weddings, departures, anniversaries, feast days, baptisms, confirmations, a new job, graduations, special achievements — each of these events is an opportunity for family members and close friends to gather together to rejoice, to show their pride in each other, to remember, and, at times, to share their sadness.

We celebrate as members of a neighbourhood, a city, and a country. Block parties, parades, Canada day fireworks, a celebration in the streets after winning the Stanley Cup — we come together to express our pride and to experience the pleasure of being with other people on a joyful occasion.

We also celebrate as members of a faith community — in parishes, schools, and homes. For Catholics, the most important celebration is Jesus himself. We come together to celebrate his life, death, and resurrection and to be nourished by his presence among us. Members of the early Christian communities were willing to risk their lives for this privilege — to come together to celebrate the Eucharist. Through our faith celebrations we deepen our relationship to God, not just as individuals, but as a believing community.

Sometimes people underestimate the importance of our human need to celebrate with others:

But when we don't take time to celebrate with others, it's easy to lose sight of who we are and what we believe in and value. Celebrations not only express our beliefs and values, but also strengthen them. We need to join with other people to remind ourselves how important some things are — family love, faith, friendship, our history, the neighbourhood community, and country in which we live.

We Support Each Other

There are times of frustration, confusion, sorrow, and pain in everyone's life. But during our worst moments, we often forget this. Because we are individuals with unique life experiences, we tend to think, "No one has ever felt this way before." It is precisely at this moment that we are most in need of the support of others.

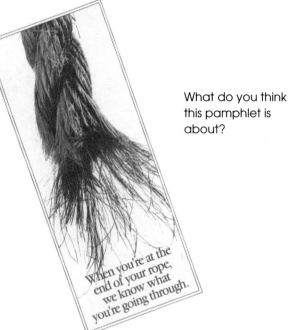

What do you think this pamphlet is about?

• Tracey and Angie have been friends for a long time, but Tracey has been at Angie's house only once. Angie usually makes some kind of an excuse.

"I can't have anyone over. My dad's sick."

Tracey knows that Angie is often upset by arguments between her parents. But what Tracey doesn't know is that Angie's father is an alcoholic. Angie is ashamed to tell Tracey, and afraid to have anyone visit her home. What if her dad is drunk? Angie loves her dad, but his alcoholism is destroying him and his family.

A few weeks ago Angie's mother got in touch with a group for the relatives of alcoholics called Al-Anon. She has gone to two meetings and discovered that she is not alone. Other people live with the same problem and feel the same desperation. Al-Anon gives Angie's mother an opportunity to share her burdens and to learn some new ways of coping.

Angie has also started to attend a group called Alateen. For the first time in her life she has found a group of people who understand what she is going through. She can say, "My father is an alcoholic, and I hate it," without shame.

*****

We receive support from many people in our lives. We cannot develop as full human beings without the love and concern of others. But there are some situations in people's lives that require a special kind of support that family members and friends may not be able to provide. This is how it was for Angie and her mother.

Groups like Al-Anon or Alateen are often referred to as *support groups* or *self-help groups*. People gather together to support each other through a difficult situation, to understand and accept their feelings, and to learn more about the nature of the problems they face. Often it is the experience of a few people that leads to the formation of a support group. For example, Bereaved Families of Ontario was formed in 1978 by three parents whose children had died. They wanted to reach out to others and share the support and comfort they found in each other. The group has grown and now provides assistance to both adults and children who have experienced the death of a family member.

When a child dies, We share the pain.

The death of a child seems so unfair... children should not die before their parents. Parents are desperately in need of help when their child dies. Their grief may be so intense that they don't understand what is happening to them. Some turn to alcohol and drug abuse. Some keep their feelings inside. Parents and their surviving children are finding the support they need by sharing their grief with other bereaved families. Bereaved Families of Ontario is here to help families cope with the painful reality of their loss and return to the mainstream of life. If you need help, want to offer financial assistance or need information for a friend, call 440-0290.

Bereaved Families of Ontario
AN ASSOCIATION OF FAMILIES WHO HAVE LOST A CHILD THROUGH DEATH

214 Merton Street, Toronto M4S 1A6.

Any change in the family is stressful. One of the most difficult situations families face is the separation of parents. Both adults and children suffer, and they experience feelings of sadness, anger, and guilt. As divorce has become more frequent, support groups for adults and children have begun. Parents gather together to share their pain, to talk about the challenges of raising children alone, and to learn from each other. Children whose parents have separated also have much in common and can be a source of comfort and support to each other. They discover that they are not alone, and that their feelings will be understood by the other members of the group.

The words at the beginning of this section could be addressed to any person facing a serious problem and needing support. They appear on a pamphlet prepared by the Alzheimer Society of Canada. Alzheimer is a disease that destroys brains cells and causes loss of memory and confusion. The families of people with Alzheimer face many problems, and they find it helpful to talk about their experiences with other people in similar situations.

All support groups have certain features in common. The members gather together to share experiences, learn from each other, feel less isolated, and gain strength from each other. At first new members may find it difficult to express their feelings or may be completely absorbed with their own grief or anger. As time goes on, they learn to accept and understand their feelings, and are able to offer comfort and support to other members.

There are many support groups that help individuals and families cope with a disease or disability.

We Create Change

Whenever there are situations that are unjust and disrespectful of human life, we have a responsibility to work for change. Sometimes we don't recognize this responsibility, or we hope that someone else will take care of the situation. We may also feel helpless — what can one person do, we wonder. But when we gather together we discover just how much we can do.

Here are just a few examples of situations that are in need of change:

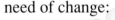

Every day all across the country, restaurants and grocery stores throw away large amounts of food. Some of this food is perishable and will spoil within a short period of time. Some of it cannot be sold because it is slightly damaged.

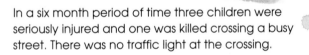

In a six month period of time three children were seriously injured and one was killed crossing a busy street. There was no traffic light at the crossing.

A thirteen-year-old girl was killed by a drunk driver who had previously been arrested four times for drunk driving. He continued on his way without stopping, and was arrested several days later. He was found guilty and was sentenced to two years in jail.

When people hear about situations like these, they often say, "That's not right. Something ought to be done." But then other matters occupy their attention, and they forget about the child who was killed crossing the street, the wasted food, or the terrible irresponsibility of the drunk driver.

But some people don't forget. They join together with others and they work for change:

• The mother of the girl who was killed saw a need for a major change in society's attitude toward drunk driving. She started an organization called Mothers Against Drunk Driving (MADD). This group educates the public about the dangers of drinking and driving, and tries to make sure that the penalties for drunk driving reflect the seriousness of the offense. Members also offer support to the families of victims of drunk driving. There is a related group for students called Students Against Drunk Driving (SADD).

• Two women decided to do something about the problem of wasted perishable food. They asked the owners of restaurants and food stores in their community if they would be willing to donate the food instead of throwing it away. Most of the people they spoke to were happy to do this, but didn't have the time or the staff to deliver the food themselves. The women offered to collect the food and take it to organizations that provide meals or give food to people each day. That was the beginning of a group called Second Harvest. Now there are many volunteer drivers who collect and deliver food all over the city.

• Residents of the neighborhood with the busy crossing organized a petition asking for a new set of traffic lights. They met with their representative on the city council, and a small group appeared at a council meeting to explain how dangerous the crossing was. They were well prepared for the meeting. They had counted the number of cars driving on the street at different times of the day, and the number of children who had crossed. They got their traffic light.

The societies we create and live in are in great need of change. Far too many people have little to eat and yet in some parts of the world we throw food away. We believe that human life is precious from the moment of conception, yet we live in a society where thousands of unborn children are destroyed each year. We are meant to be caretakers of the physical environment, yet we pollute and create unnecessary garbage.

When we gather together we discover just how much we can do. Demonstrations, boycotts, petitions, education for the public, lobbying the government to change unjust laws — these are only some ways people bring about change.

It is easy to get discouraged. That is why prayer within our faith community is so important. When we gather together for the Eucharist we pray for the strength and wisdom to create a society that reflects God's plan for creation.

We Work Together

"Work is love made visible." (Kahlil Gibran)

"Work is not a curse, it is a blessing from God."
(Pope John Paul II)

"When love and skill work together, expect a
masterpiece." (John Ruskin)

"No nation can prosper till it learns that there is as
much dignity in tilling a field as in writing a poem."
(Booker T. Washington)

"No one has a right to sit down and feel hopeless.
There's too much work to do." (Dorothy Day)

"It is a sublime mystery that Christ should begin to work
before he began to teach; a humble workman before
being the teacher of all nations." (Pope Pius XII)

Work is an essential part of being human; it is something we share with each other. All over the world — in offices, homes, fields where food is grown, factories, classrooms, small and large stores — people are using their intelligence, their talents, their knowledge, and their energy. Through their work, whether in small or large groups, they are continuing God's work of creation.

Work is always a co-operative enterprise. Each person has a contribution to make and depends on the work of every other member of the group. This is true whether it's a small group of students, a large factory or business, a research team, or a city with thousands of employees.

• Mr. Dryden's class has been studying the lifestyle of families in the past — native, pioneer, and immigrant families. Small groups of students are preparing presentations on the way children were raised, roles of men and women, preparation of food, clothing, education, housing, and recreation.

One group is made up of Bill, Angie, and Mark. Angie wasn't pleased when Mr. Dryden asked her to work with Bill and Mark. "Bill won't do any work, and Mark will spend his time fooling around," she complained. "Bill's a terrific artist, and Mark's very imaginative," Mr Dryden remarked.

The group worked together better than Angie expected. Bill researched the types of houses and made a series of drawings. Angie did more reading than Mark, but Mark used her notes to prepare imaginary scenes from early pioneer life. He persuaded Angie and Bill to act out these scenes as part of the presentation.

138

• In a large city, the workers who collect garbage have gone on strike. Special areas in the parks have been set up as temporary collection sites. When garbage was being collected regularly, people rarely thought about the workers who performed this service, but now it's a big topic of conversation.

Sometimes it takes a crisis for us to realize how much we depend on the work of others.

• A team of scientists discovered the location on the chromosome of a gene that is responsible for a serious inherited disease. When the doctor who headed the research team was interviewed, she explained that the discovery was really the work of thousands of people. "Thousands? That's a very large research team," the interviewer commented. "The team has only six members," the doctor explained, "but by themselves, they could never have accomplished the work."

Each medical discovery is the work of many people: other doctors involved in similar projects who share their work, teachers who inspire people to go into medical research, family members of research teams who provide support and encouragement, patients who participate in projects, people who raise money for research, hospital workers who answer the phone, clean the laboratory and prepare meals.

Each of these stories demonstrates how much we depend on each other. Even when people are working alone, they are still part of a group of workers. The book you read to prepare a school assignment reflects the effort of hundreds of people. They become part of your life through their work. The homework you do is not just a personal obligation, but a responsibility as a member of a classroom. When you are prepared for class, you are a fully contributing member of the group — able to answer questions, share the results of your work, and offer your opinions in a discussion.

There are many times when work is difficult, boring, and unappealing. But if we remember that we are not working alone, it helps us accept the challenge and the difficulties. Our contribution is needed in the family, in the classroom, in the church, in the community, and in all of human society. We join together to share our talents, to serve each other, and to participate in the redemption of the world.

Belonging to the Group

Much earlier you discussed the social environment and its powerful influence on people. Whenever people are gathered together, they create a social environment. No matter what they are doing — celebrating at a party, working on a construction site, participating in a discussion in the classroom, having a meeting in an office, practising for a school concert — each member of the group contributes to the creation of this social environment. In other words, membership in a group is not only an opportunity to belong, to share experiences, and to work together; it is also a personal responsibility.

What are the responsibilities involved in belonging to a group?

3) Resolving conflicts fairly

1) Commitment to the group

2) Good communication

5) Generosity in sharing talents and other resources

6) Respect for the rules of the group

4) Active participation

When all members of a group accept these responsibilities, they create a social environment that is a positive influence in each of their lives.

Many different circumstances bring people together. Sometimes membership in a group is by choice; other times it is not. It's not difficult to be committed to people whom we like and with whom we share a common interest. But the challenge for all of us is to create a true spirit of community whenever we come together with others.

Good communication, a fair resolution of conflicts, commitment, generosity, active participation, respect for rules — these are all indications that the spirit of community exists within a group. But there are two signs of community that are absolutely essential:

• the group respects and appreciates the uniqueness of each individual
• the group is more concerned with including others than with excluding.

In order to understand why these two signs of community are so important, we need to go back to the first question in this book — what does it mean to be a person? To be a person is:

- to be a physical-spiritual creature made in the image of God
- to live in relationship with other people
- to experience limitations and failures
- to be so loved that God became one of us to show us how to be human
- to be a deep and wonderful mystery.

Respect and appreciation for each unique individual is based on this understanding of what it means to be a person. We share our human nature with every person in the world. Our appearance, talents, interests, personalities, achievements, abilities, and experiences differ, but not our fundamental humanity.

Because the world we live in is so complex, we have a strong inclination to make things simpler than they are. Instead of respecting the uniqueness of each person, we try to fit them into categories: nerds, jocks, popular people, people who wear the right clothes, people who get good marks, the in-group, the out-group. The human mind is very good at creating and understanding categories.

But when we try to understand people in this way, we run into trouble. We forget that we share a common human nature. We create special categories for people who are "in" and people who are "out." We create groups that are more concerned with excluding others than with including them. The result can be a serious human failing that we call *prejudice*.

Prejudice is a positive or negative attitude (but we usually use the word to mean a negative attitude) toward individuals or groups that is based on differences related to a person's appearance, race, religion, sex, nationality, age, education, wealth, or social status.

Another word that is often used when we talk about prejudice is *discrimination*. When we discriminate against people, we don't just notice their differences, but we allow these differences to guide our attitudes and actions. For example, we refuse to allow someone into a group because of the way he or she dresses. Or we act as if people of a different race or religion do not have the same human feelings, needs, concerns, and hopes that we have.

A true spirit of community and prejudice cannot exist together. When we discriminate, we break the commandment that Jesus gave us to love one another. We have a deep need to belong to groups, but these groups have to reflect our values and our understanding of what it means to be a person. When they do not, their influence is destructive. Each member of the group is diminished.

Only when we remember how much we have in common, can we create a social environment where individuals are respected, appreciated, and welcomed because each one of them reflects the mystery of God. It is this spirit of community in families, parishes, classrooms, neighbour-hoods, clubs, teams, and work places that allows people who are part of these groups to continue to grow and become more fully human.

Sylvia Santin: pp. 14; 33 (left column second from top);
Canadian Special Olympics: pp. 21; 129 (top row middle);
Canapress: pp. 129 (right column third from top); 136 (bottom right);
Robert and Marina Wengert: p. 36;
John Mastromatteo: p. 136 (top);
Stephen Brown: p. 129 (bottom right);
Second Harvest: p. 135 (left);
MADD: p. 135 (right);
Canada Packers: p. 137 (top left);
The Kidney Foundation of Canada: p. 49;
Blissymbolics Communication International and Sarah Mathews: p. 50;
Catholic News Service/Reynolds: p. 51;
Canadian Sport Parachuting Association: p 127.

p. 62: "Great Things Have Happened" from *An Exchange of Gifts* by Alden Nowlan. Reprinted with the permission of Stoddart Publishing Co. Limited.